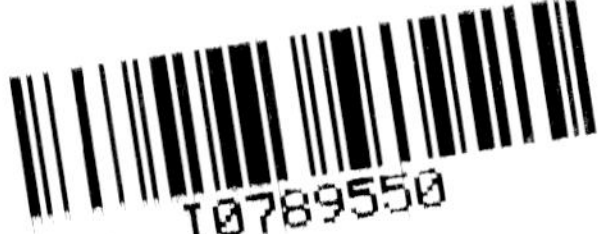

Coloring book for kids ages amazing rabbit image for design

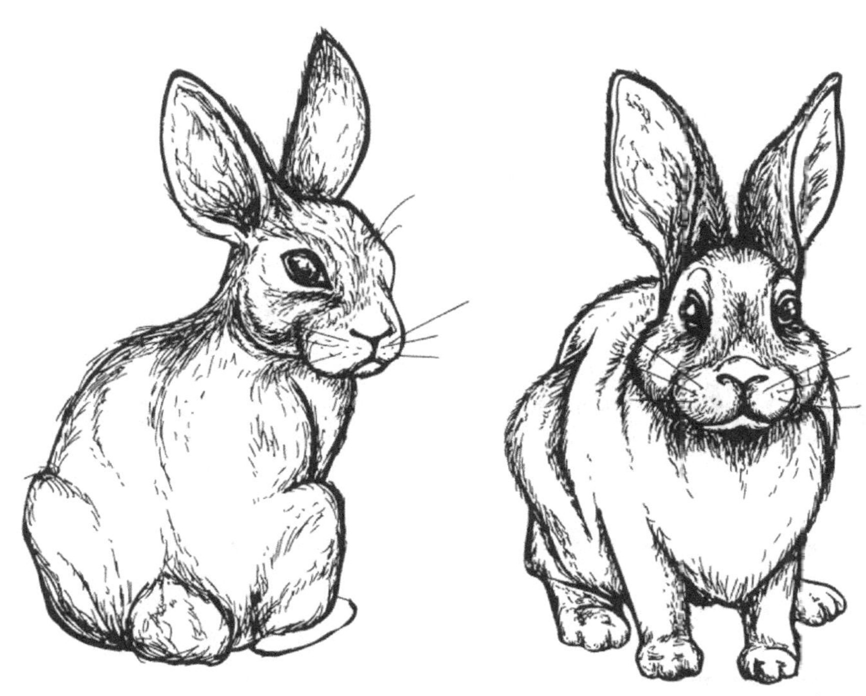

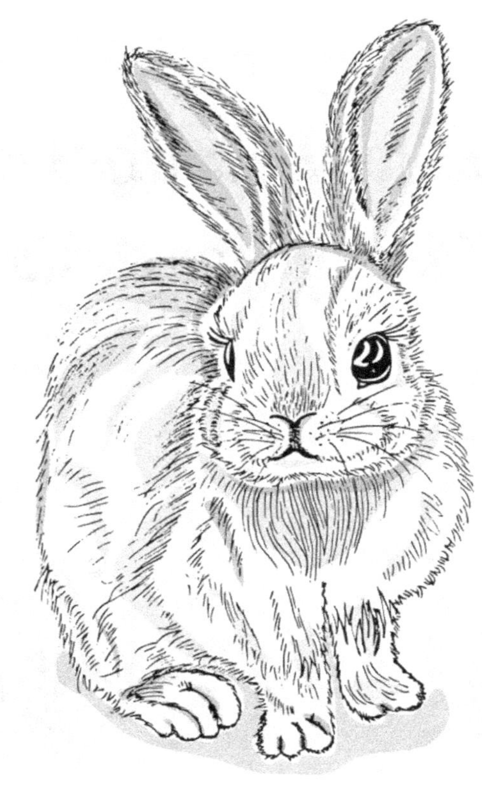

This coloring book is belongs to

____

____

____

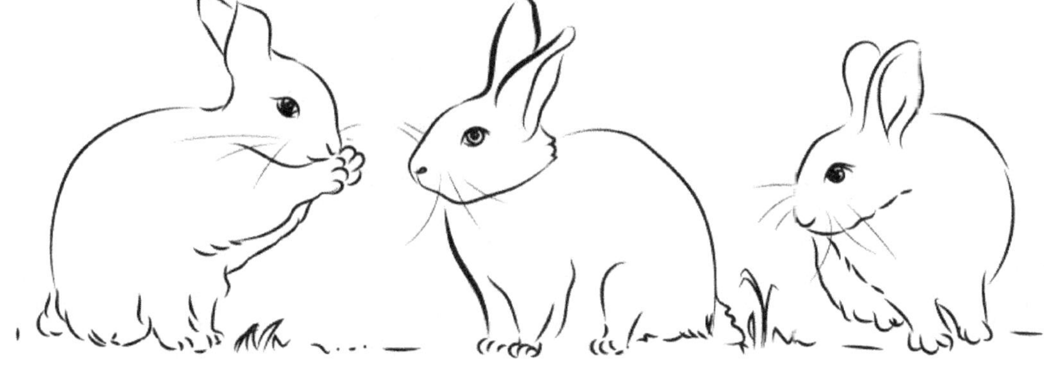

Alice in Wonderland

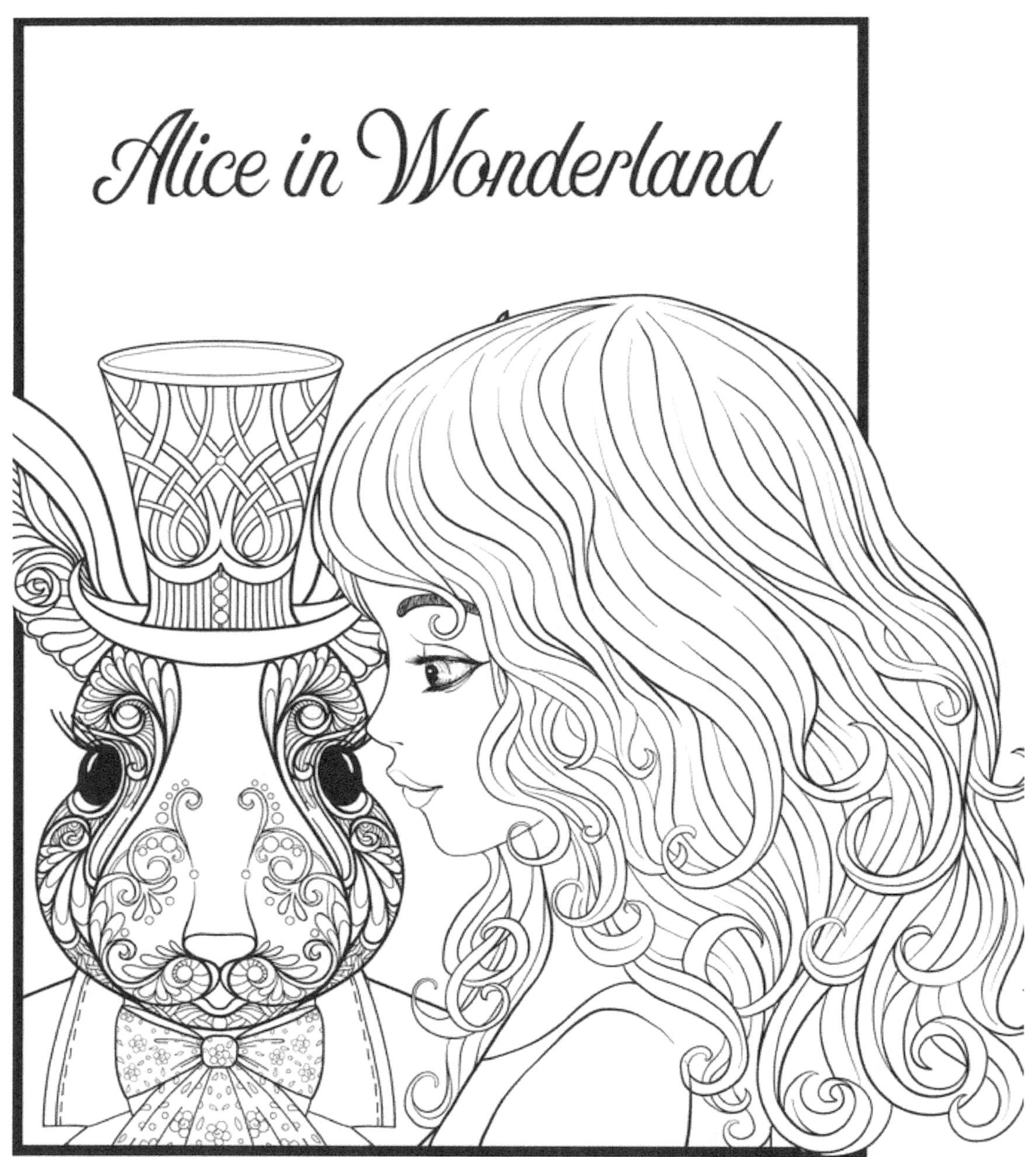

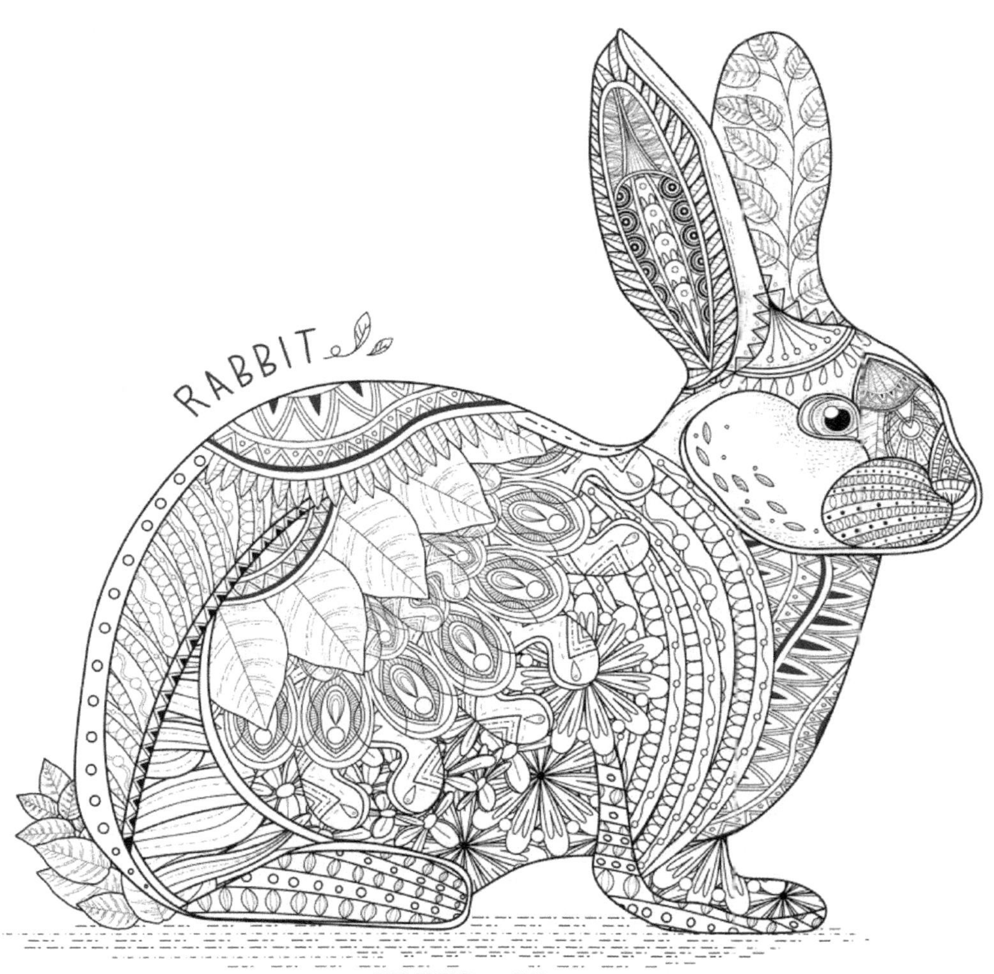
RABBIT

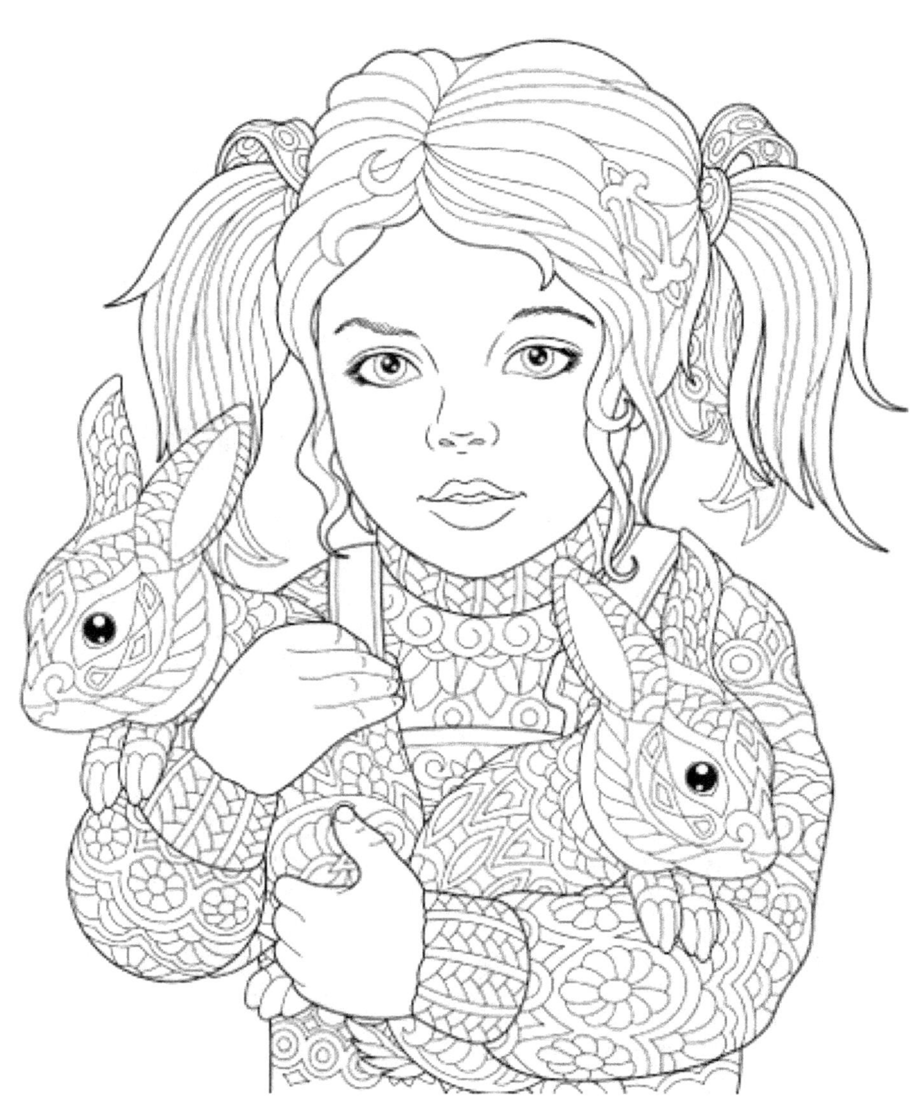

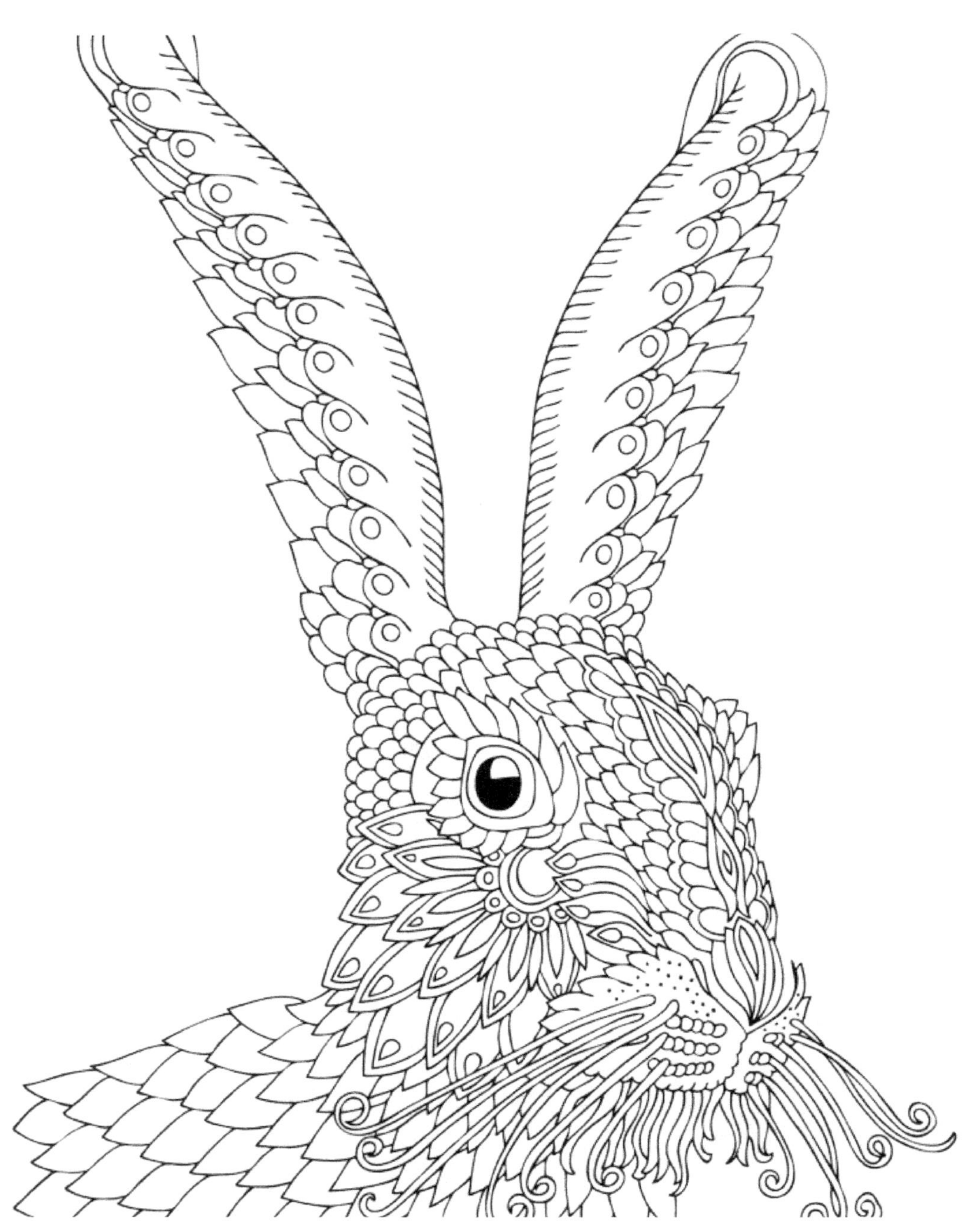

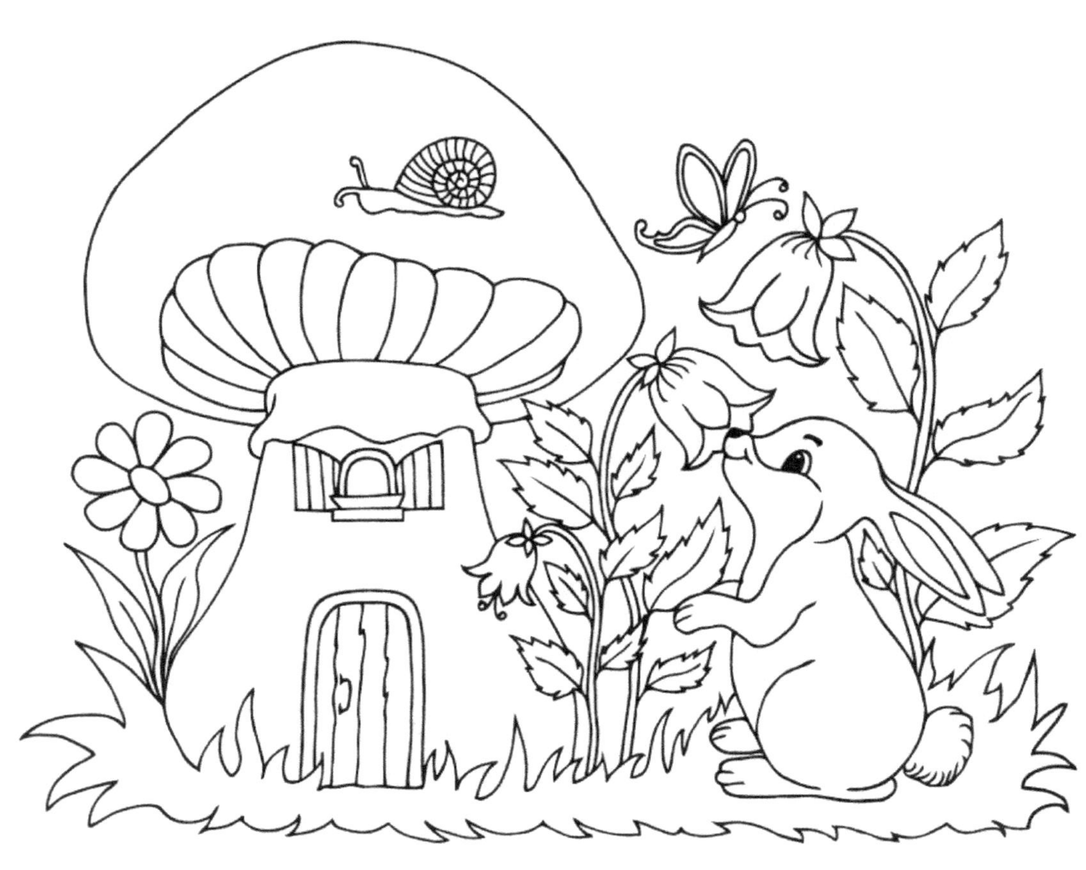

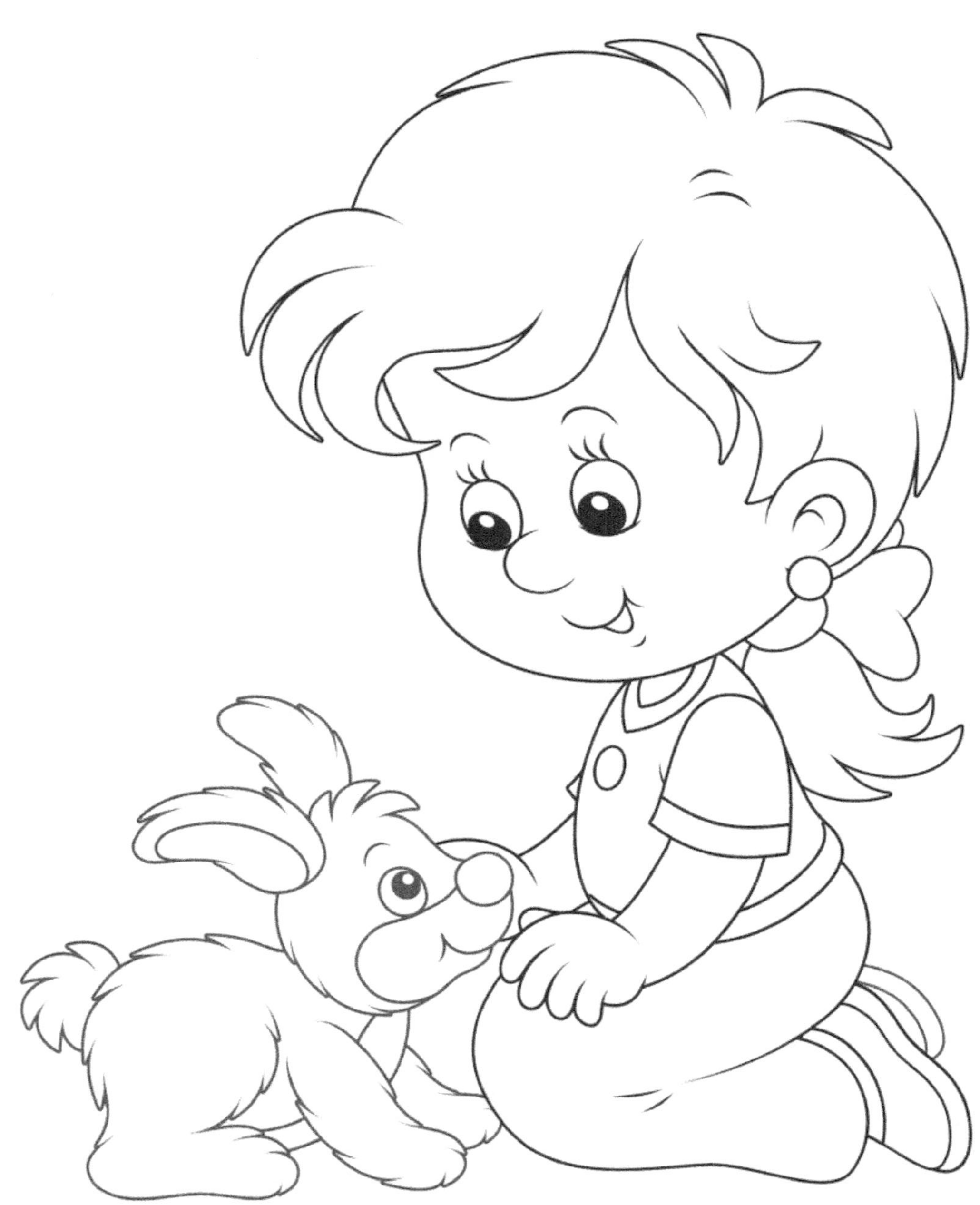

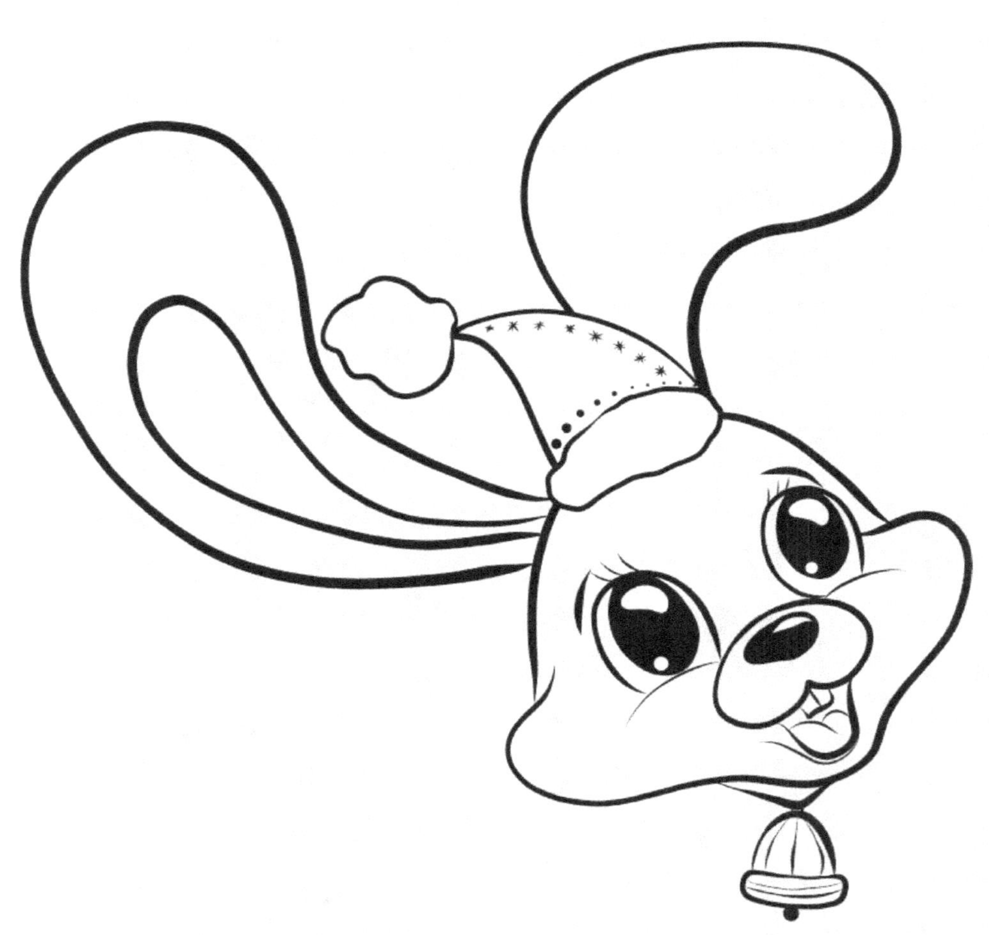

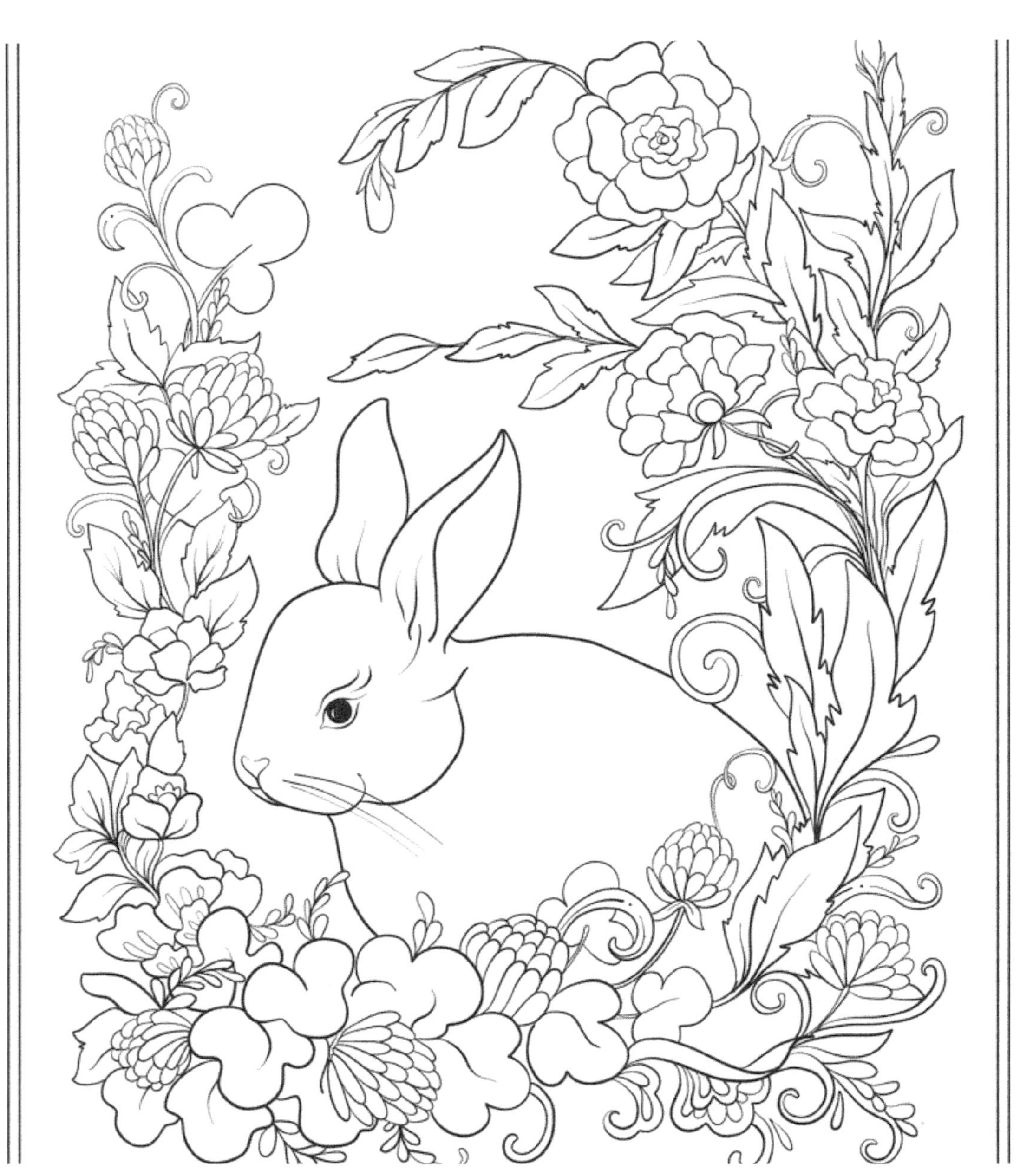

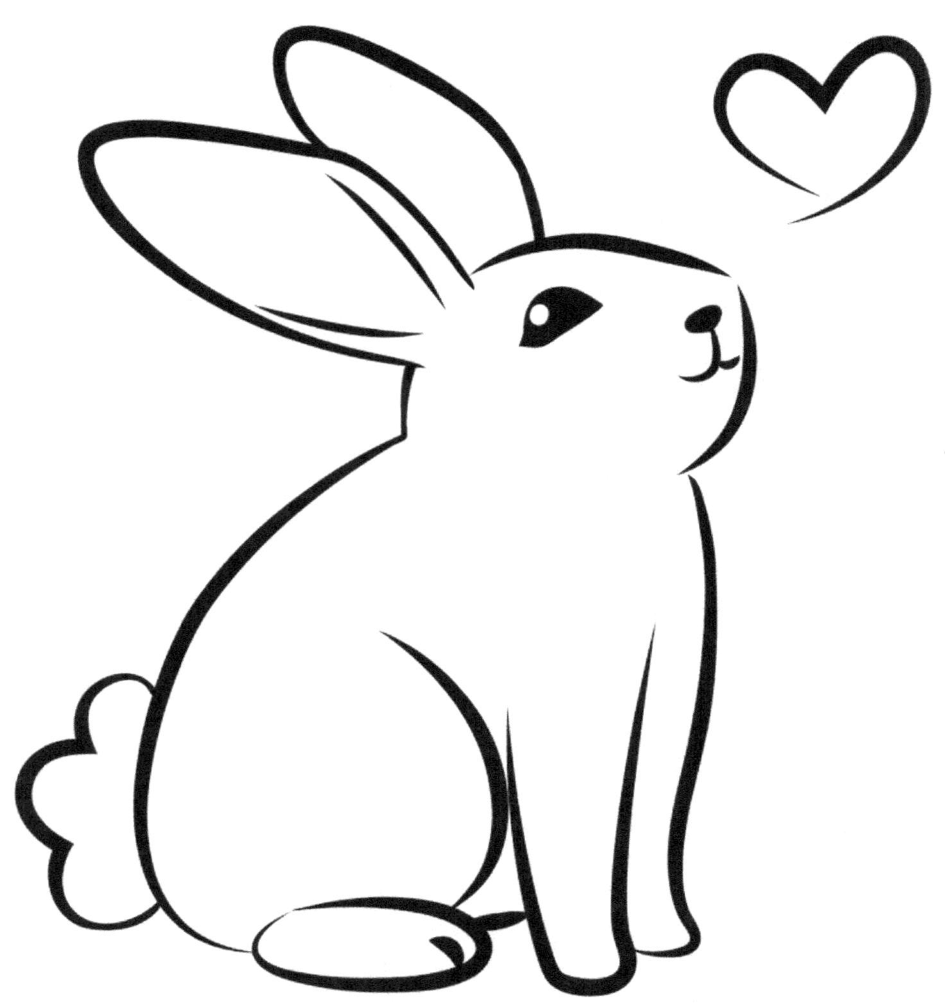

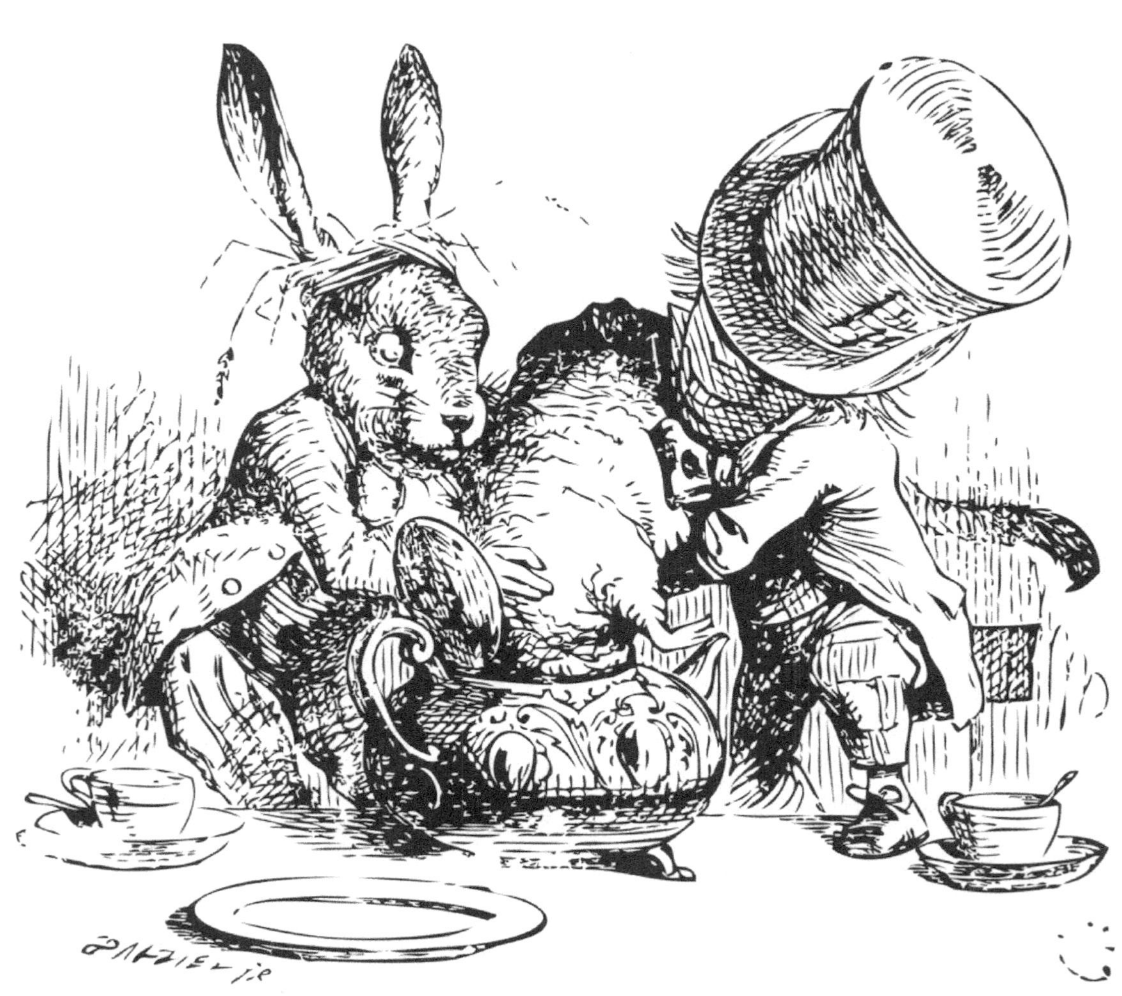

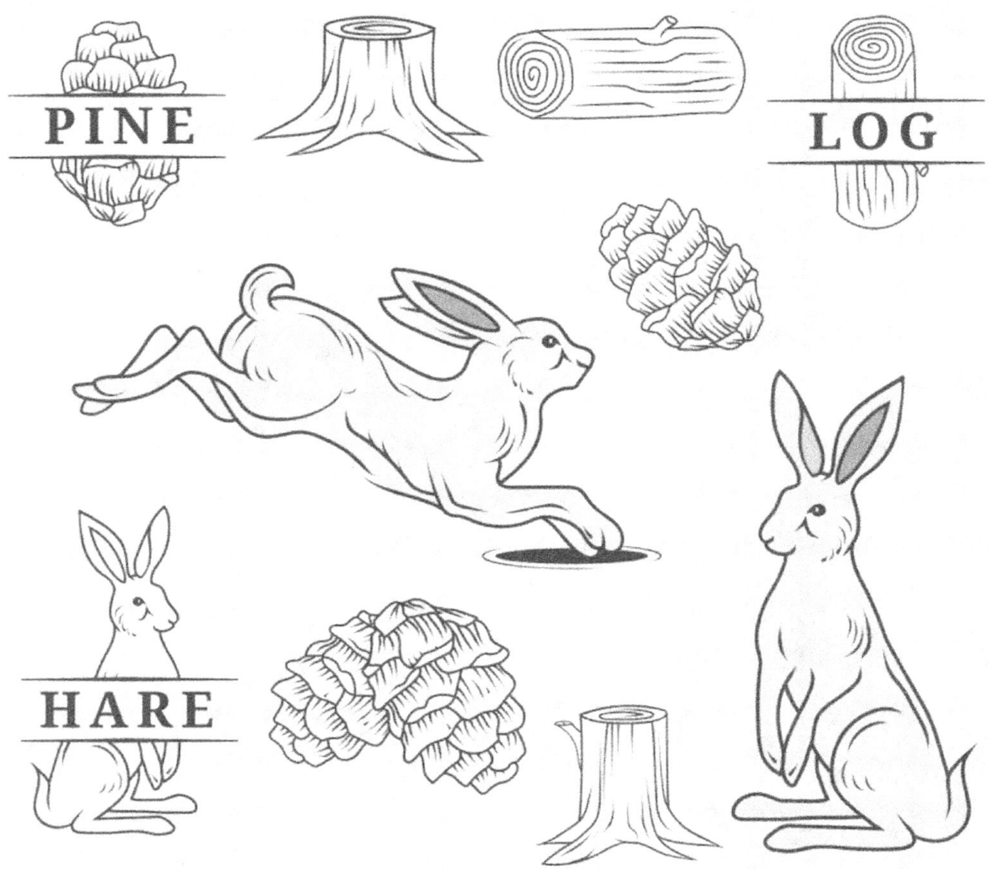
PINE
LOG
HARE

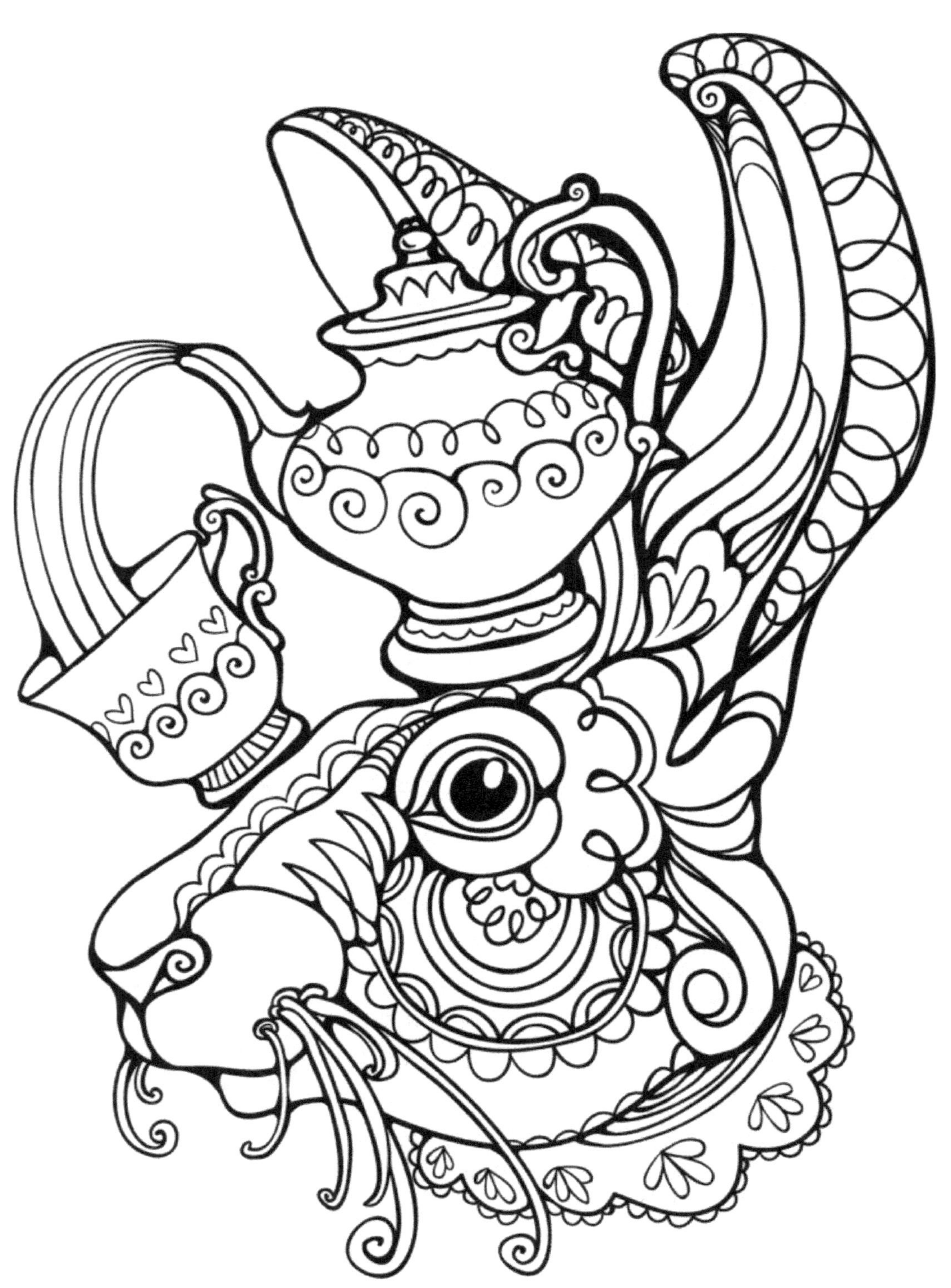

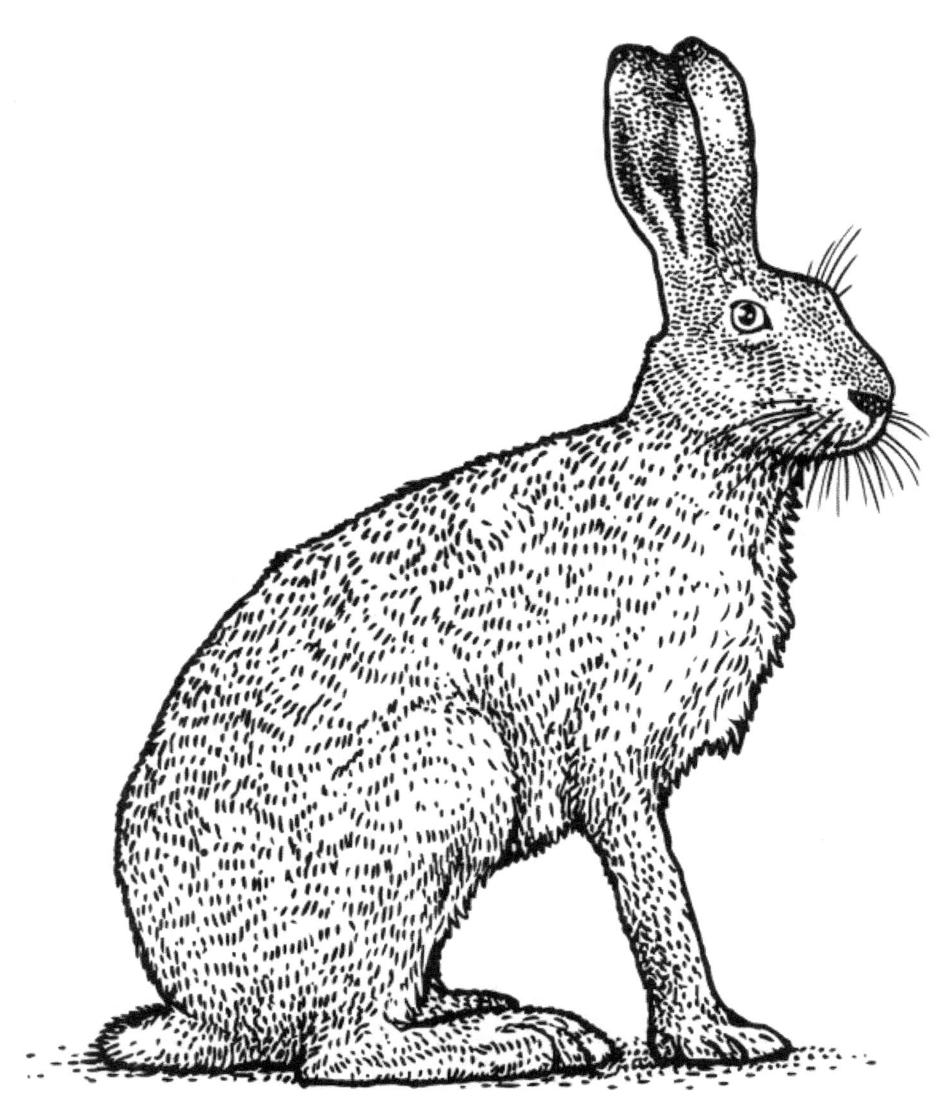

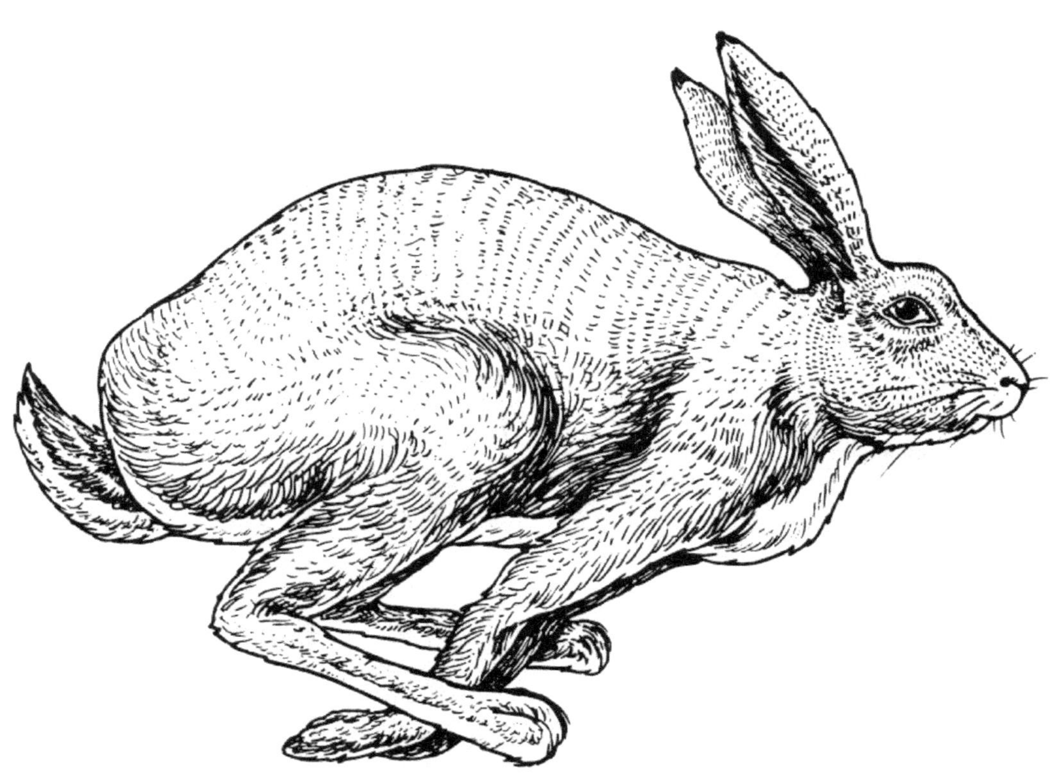

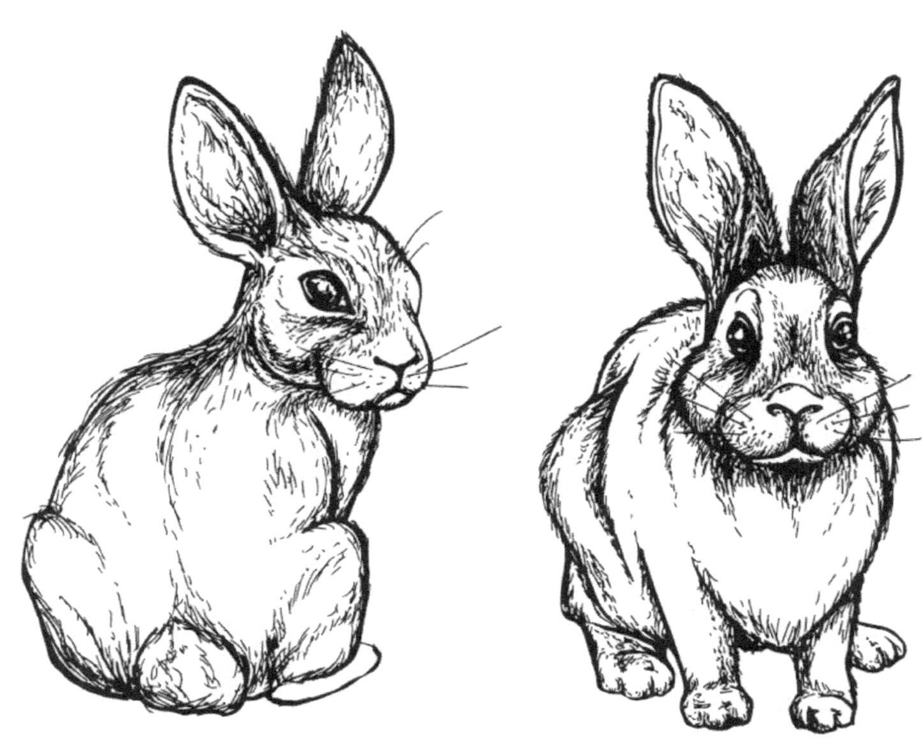

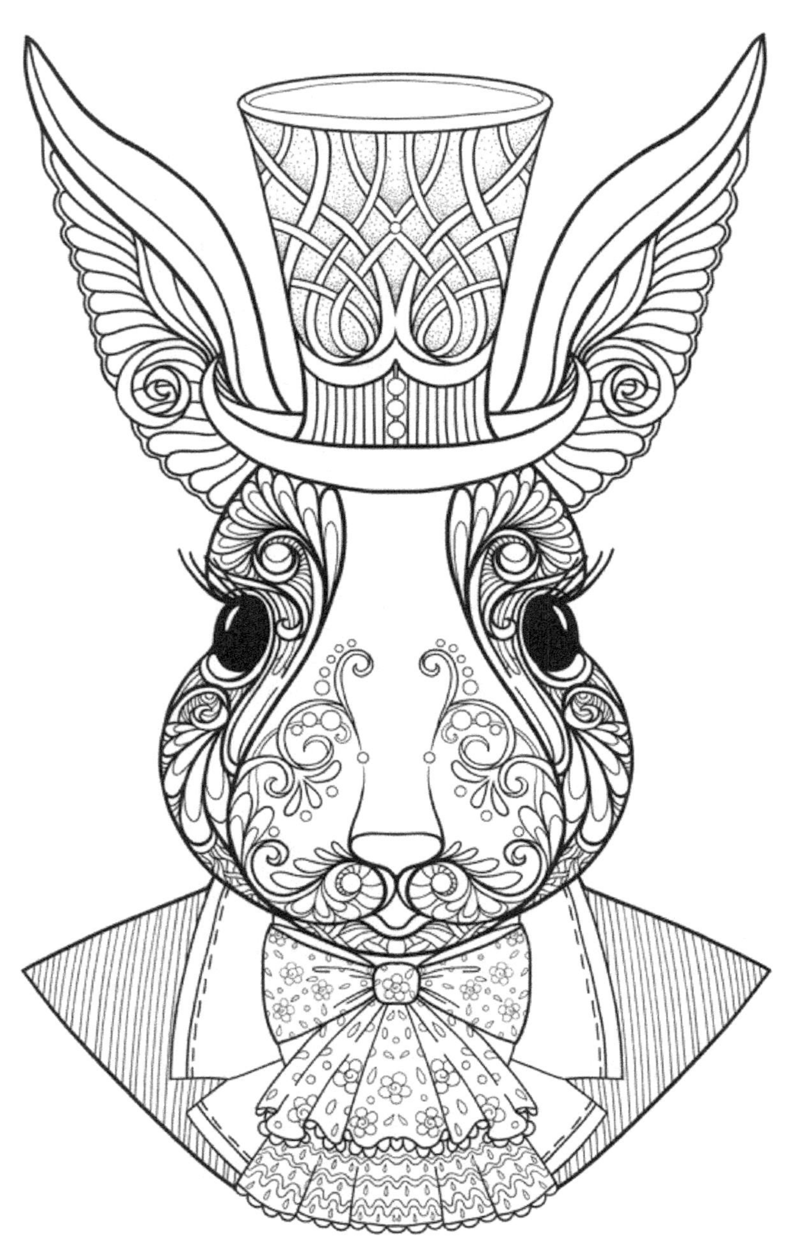

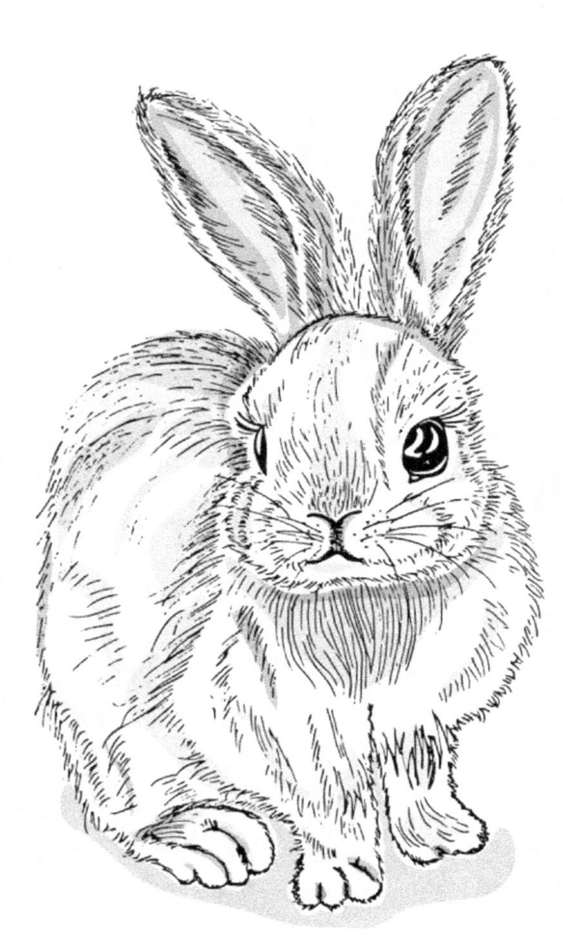

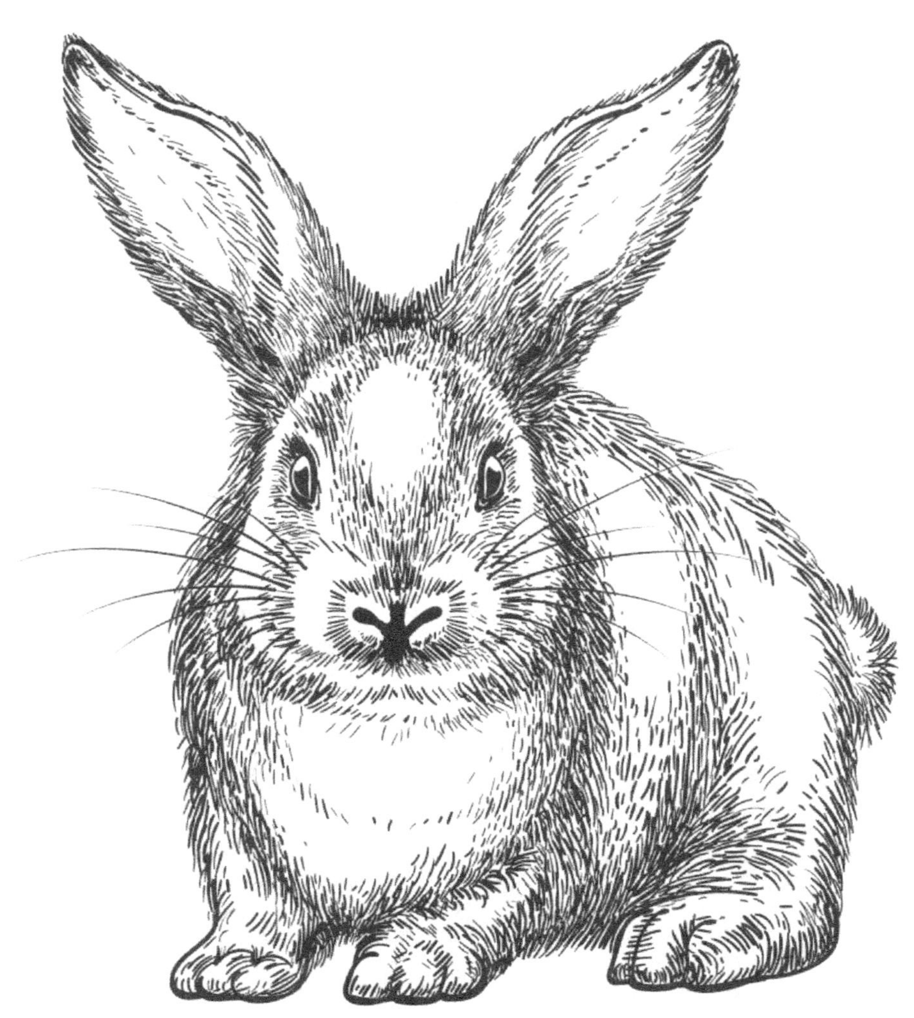

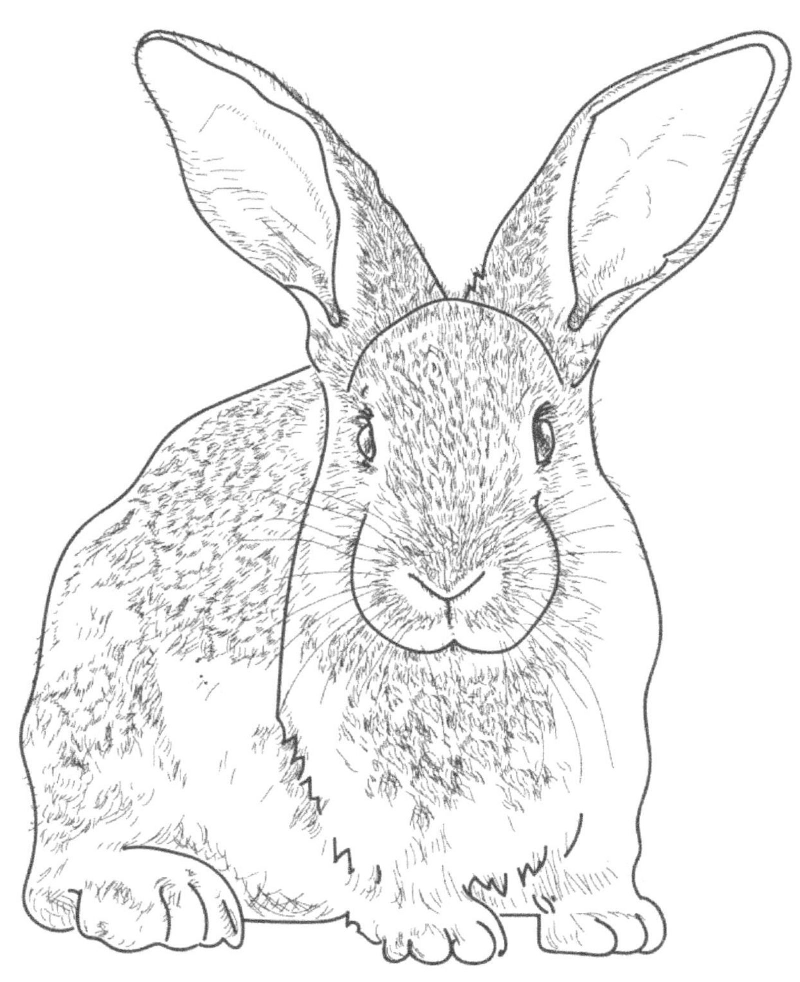

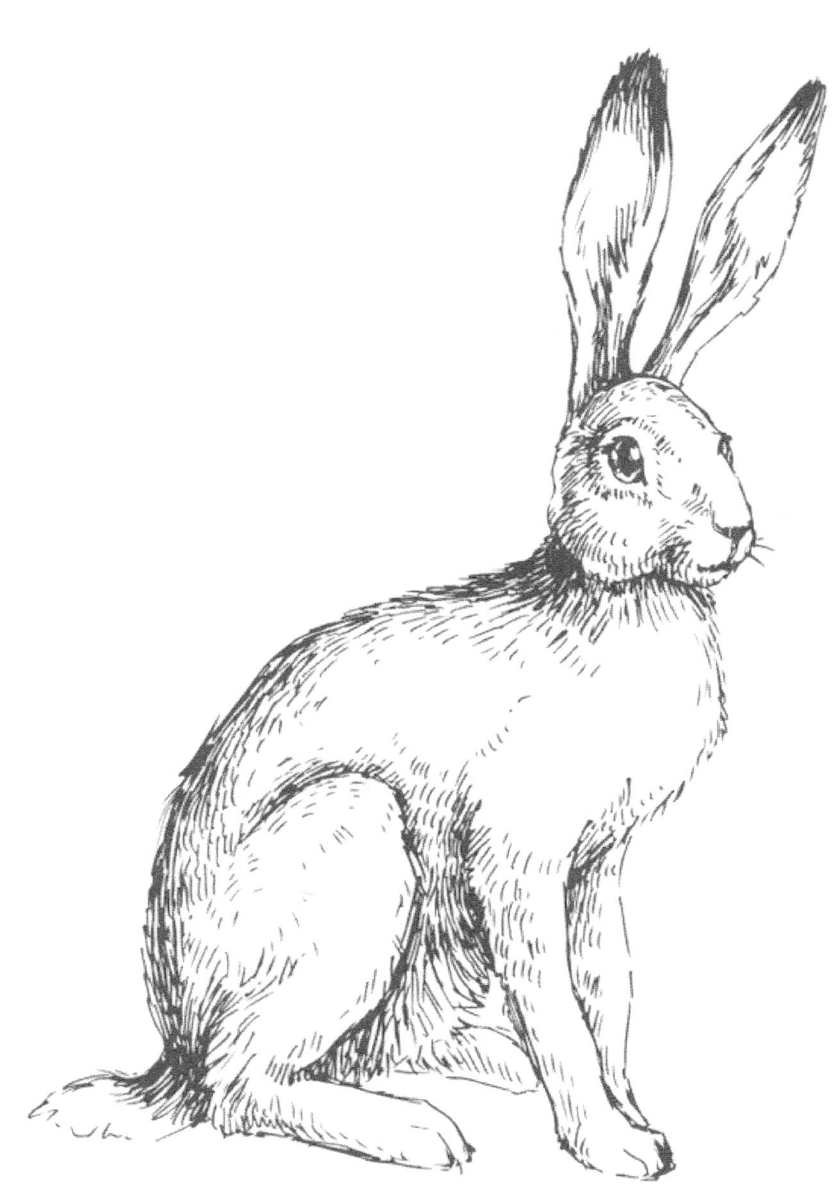

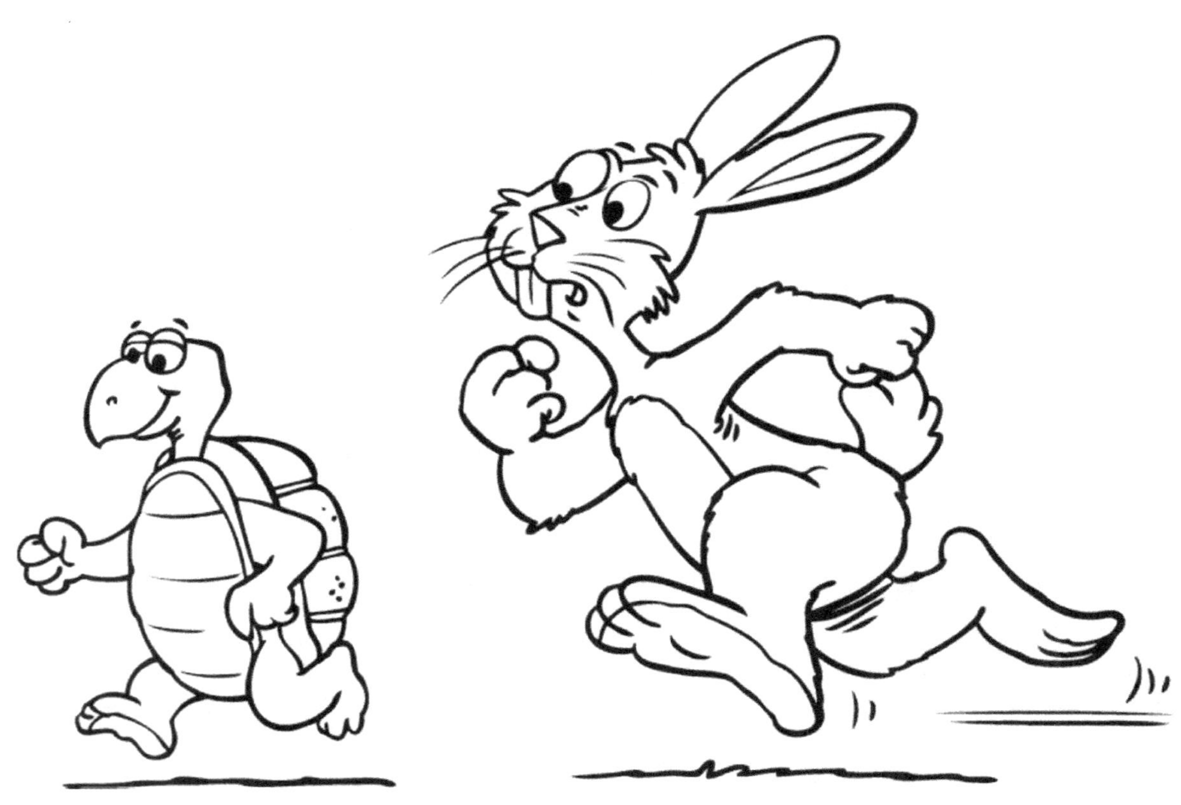

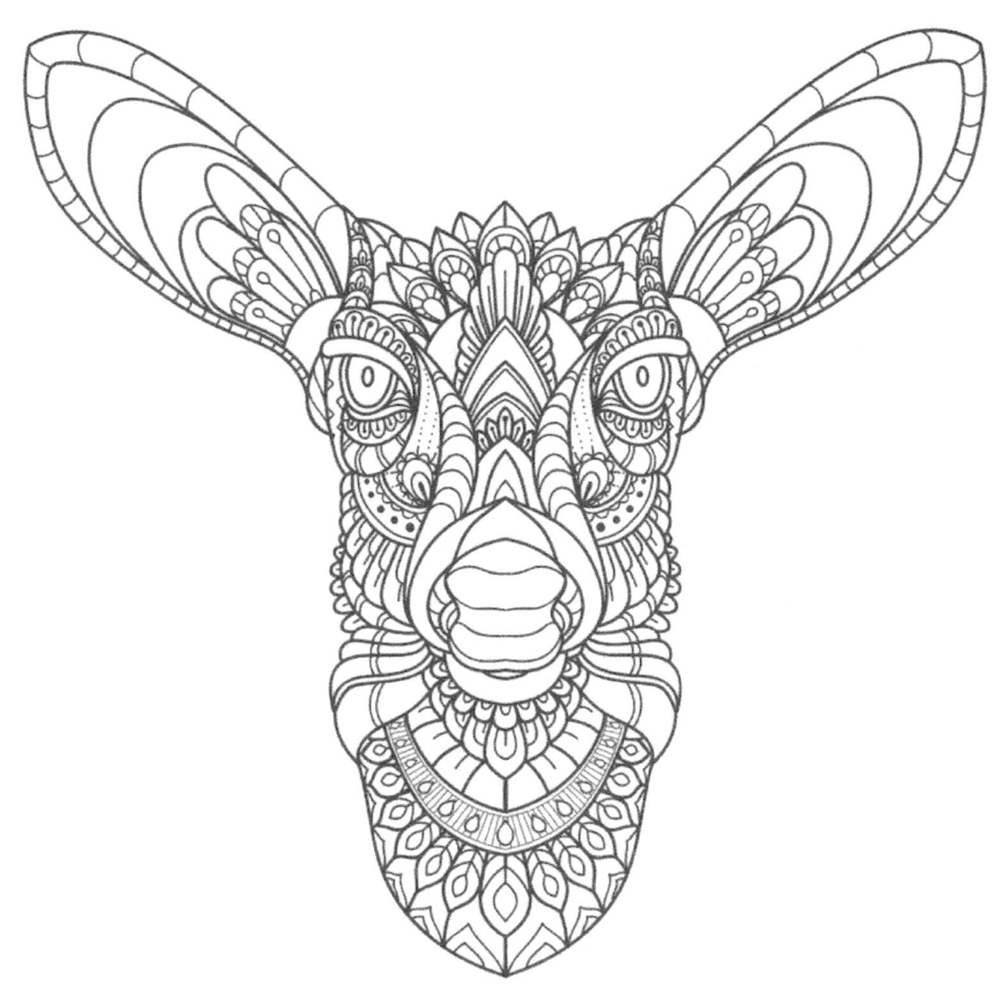

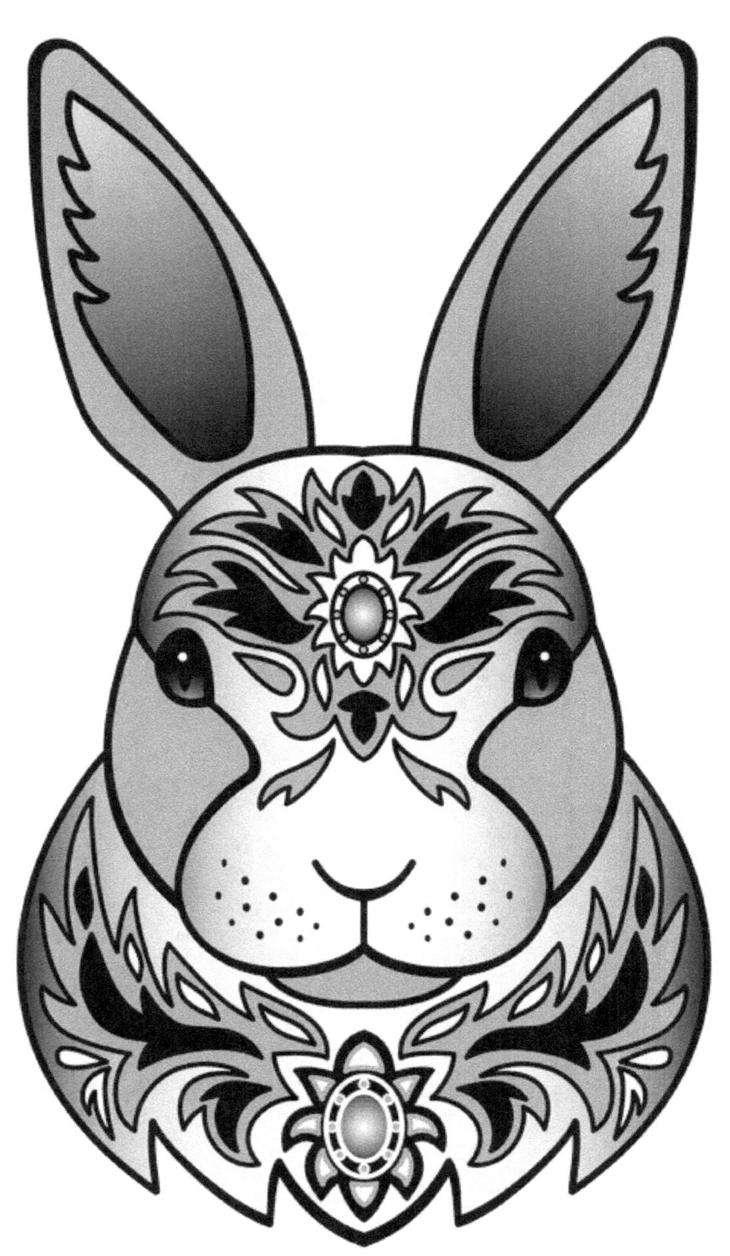

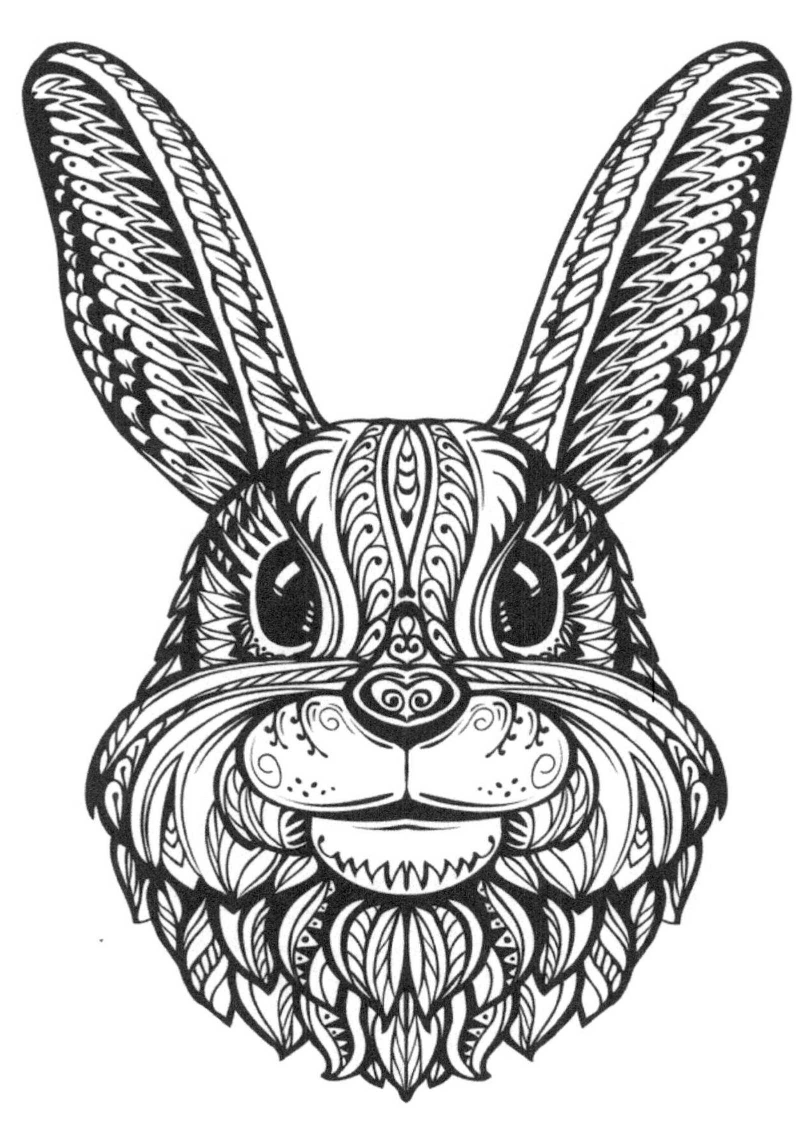

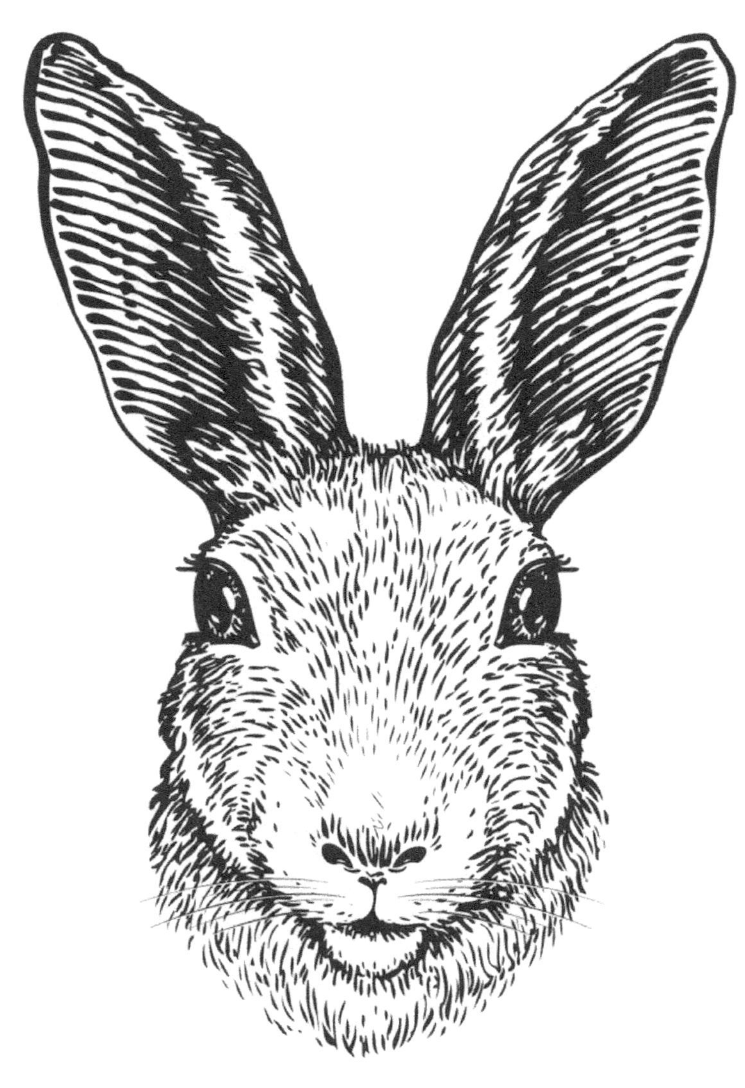

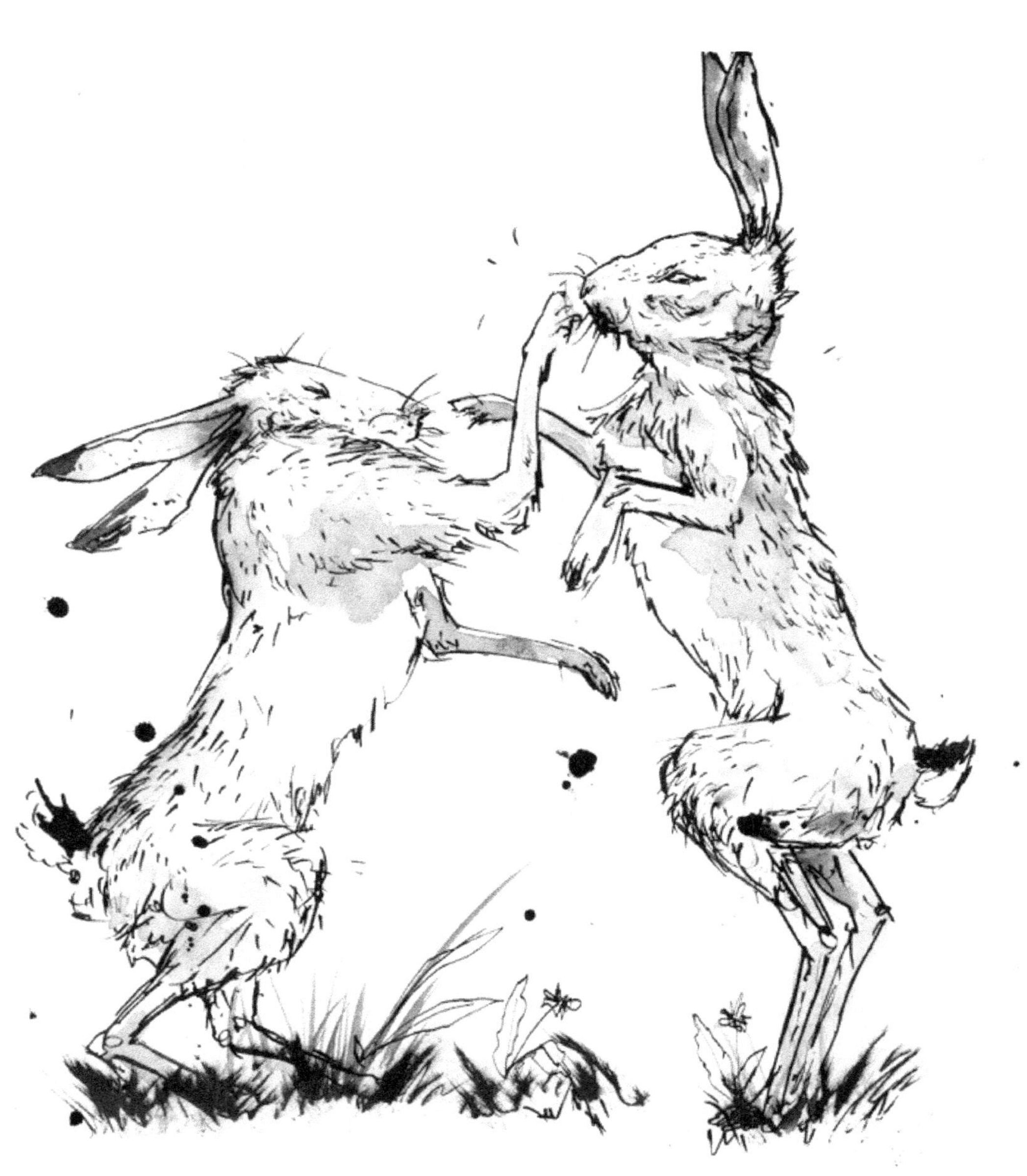

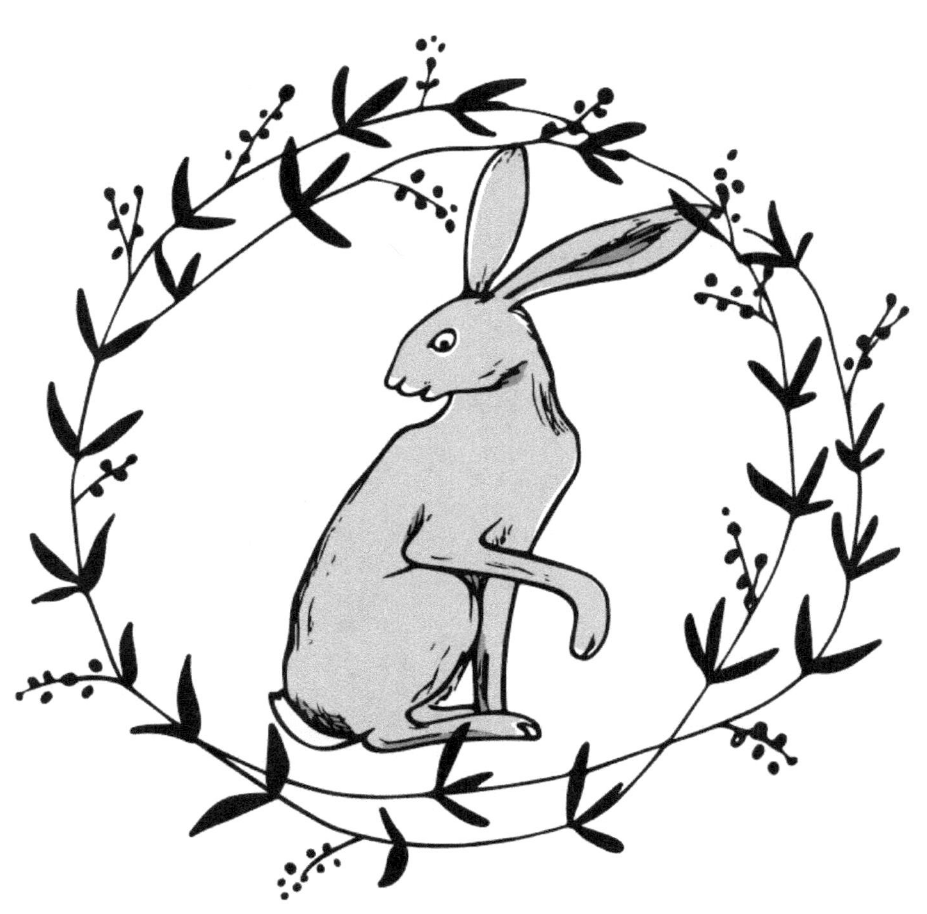

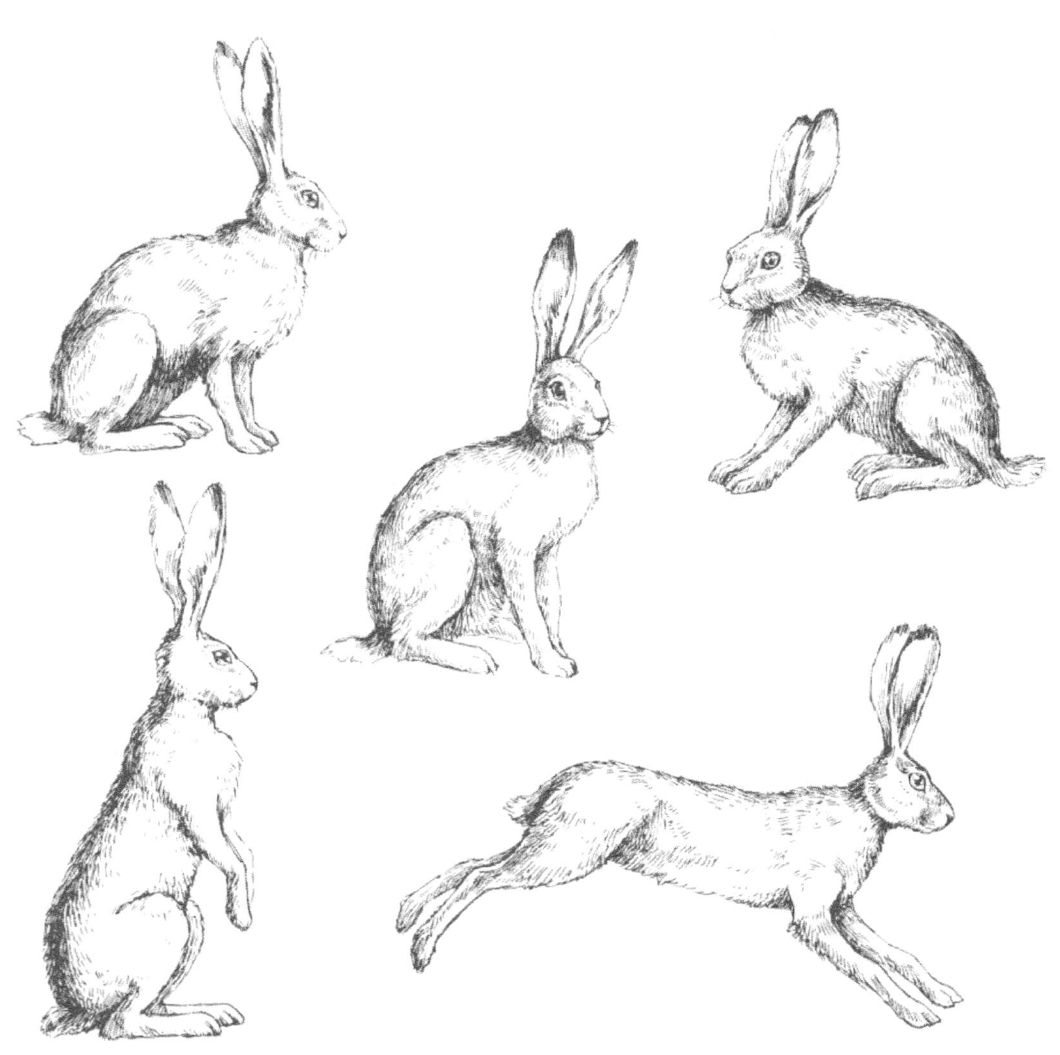

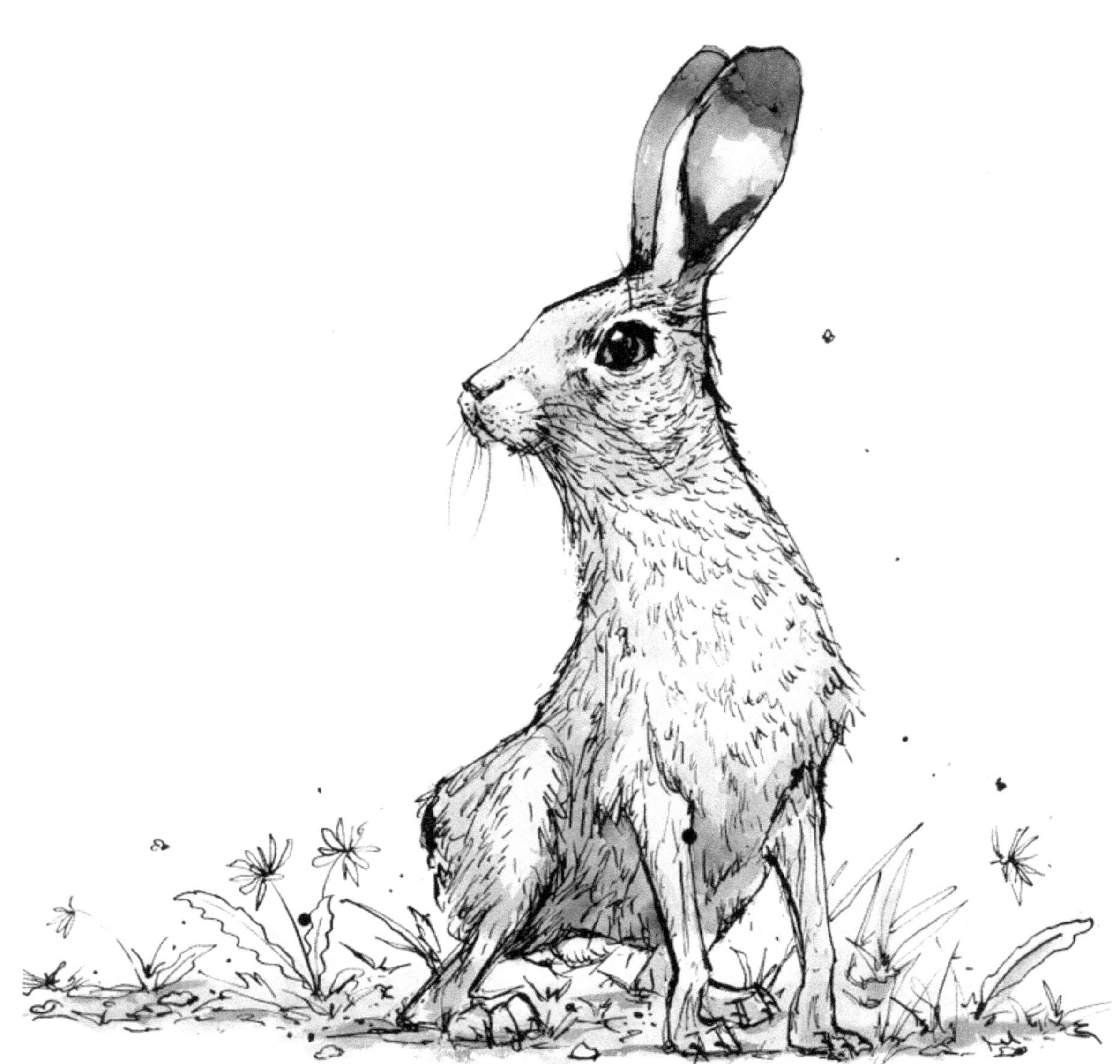

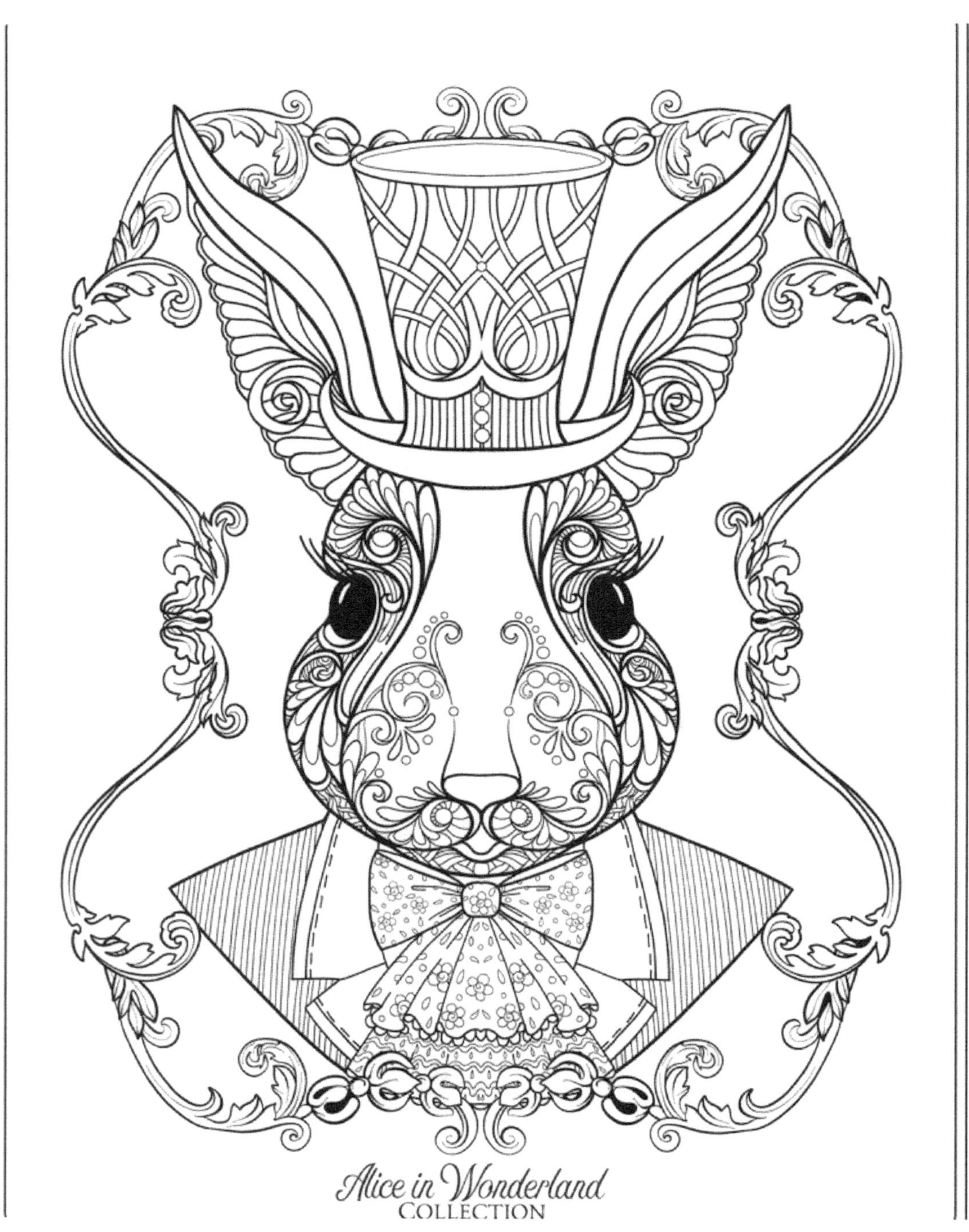

Alice in Wonderland
COLLECTION

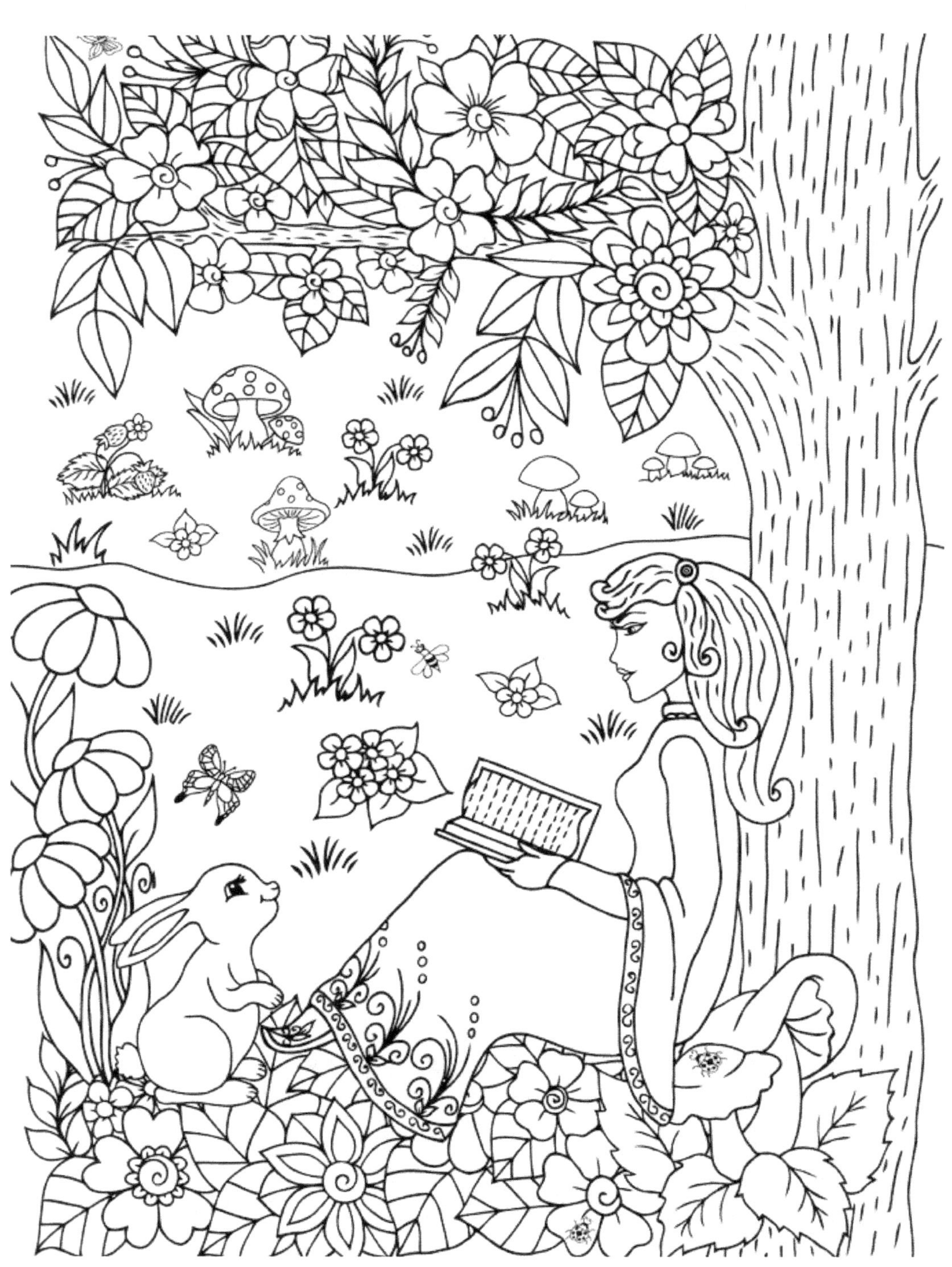

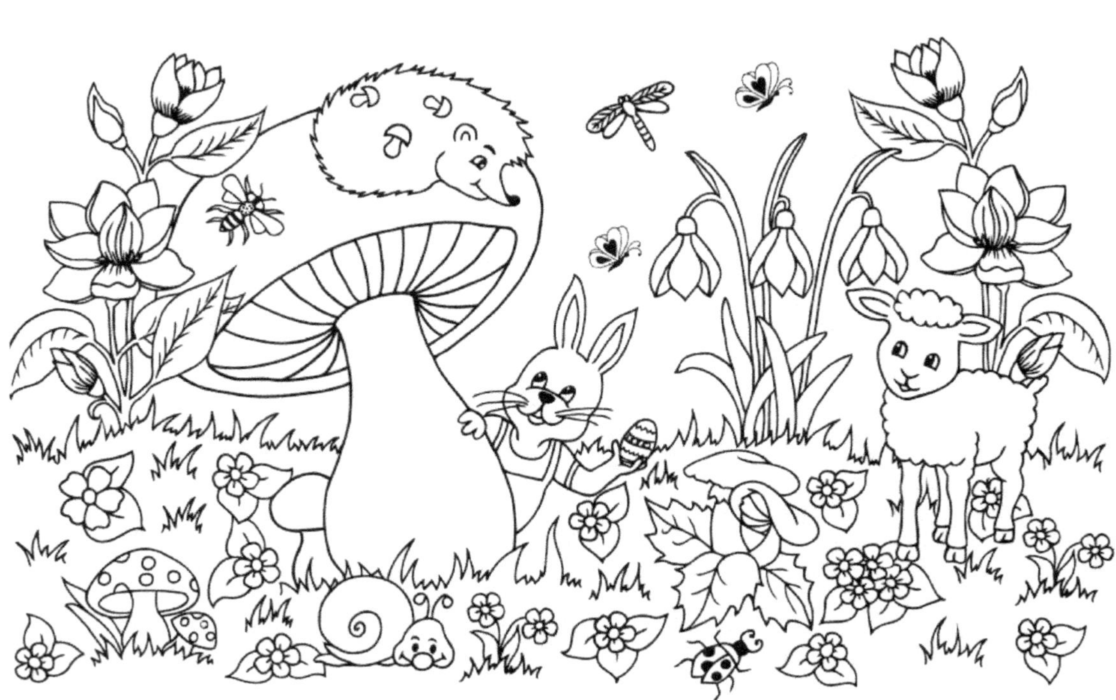

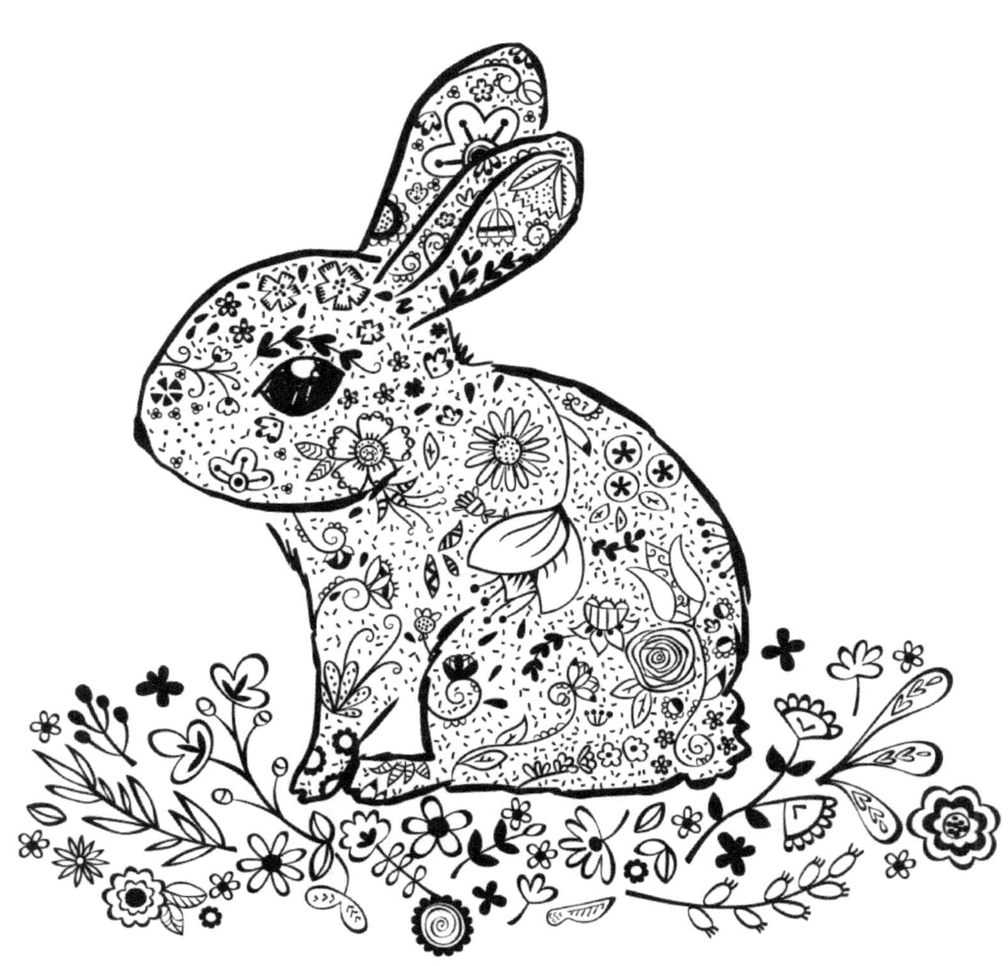

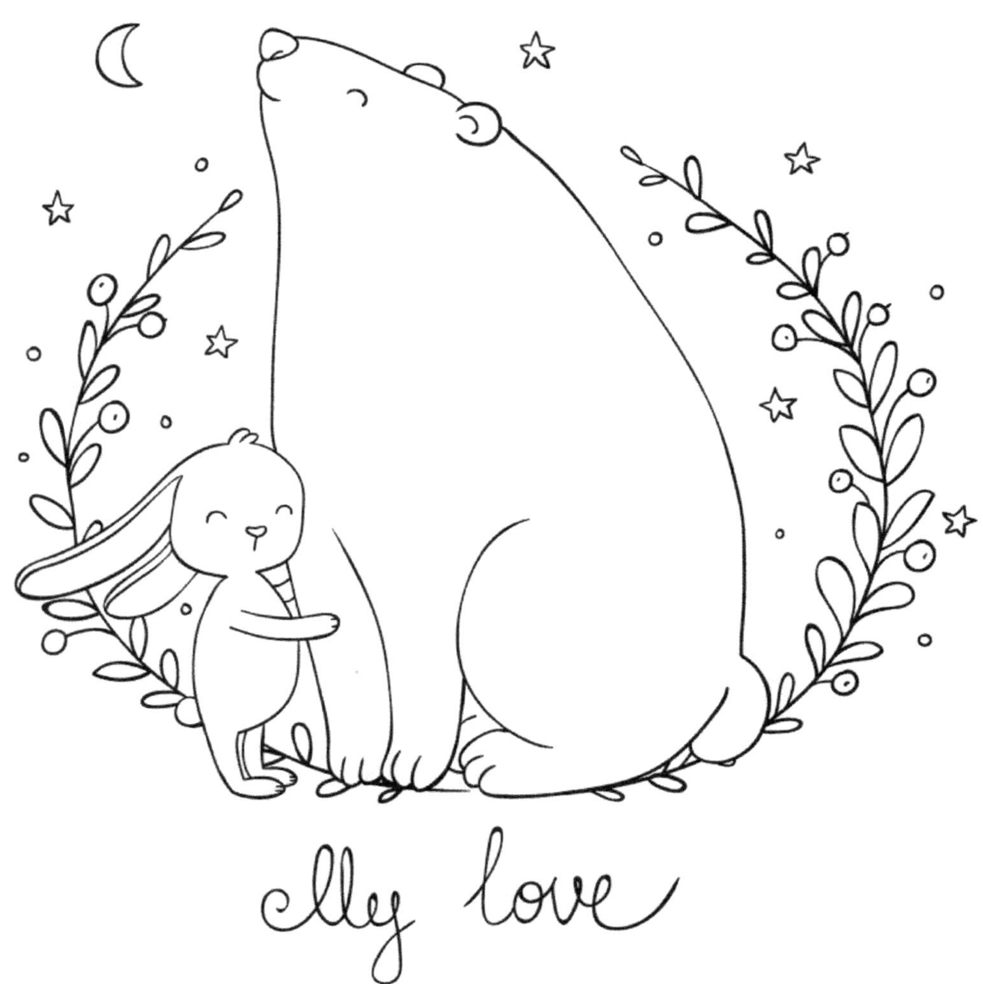

My love

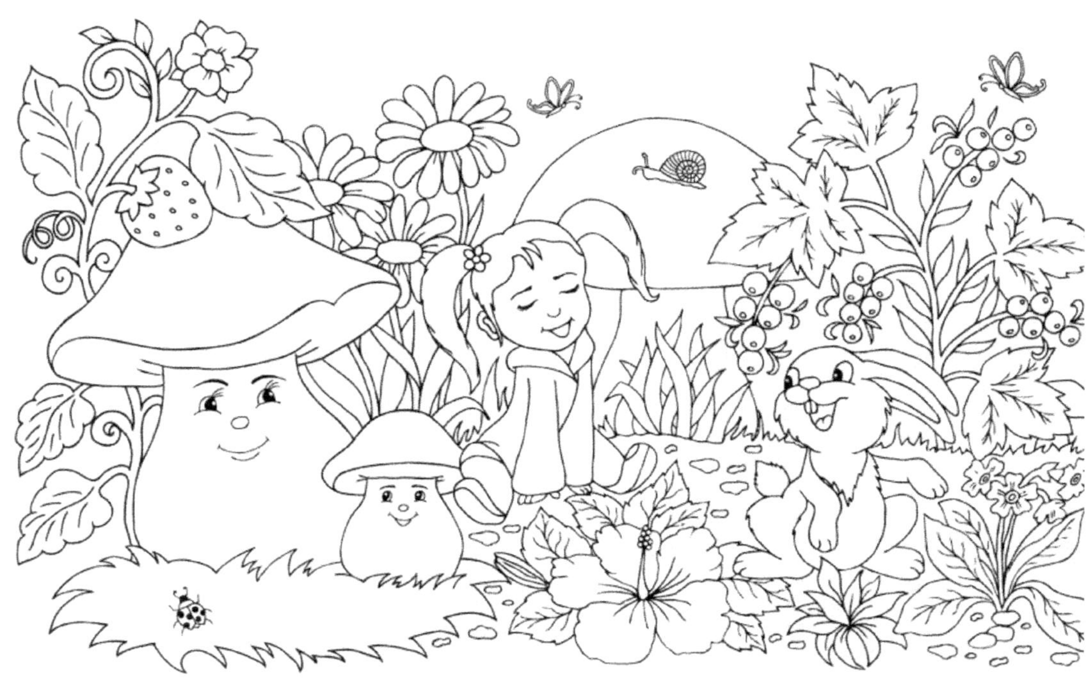